Y. M. C. A. GRADUATE SCHOOL

STUDIES IN SOCIAL AND RELIGIOUS ENGINEERING

Survey of the Negro Boy Life in Nashville   SYMPOSIUM
What Is Boys' Work?   WALTER L. STONE
Coming to Terms with the Universe   E. MCNEIL POTEAT, JR.
*A Source Book on the Church and the Negro Before 1865   W. D. WEATHERFORD
A Sociological Case Study of a Gang   WALTER L. STONE
Is God a Person?   EDGAR S. BRIGHTMAN
A Camp Counselor's Manual   WALTER L. STONE
*Whither Bound   JOHN A. MACKAY
Rethinking the Y. M. C. A.   JUDSON G. ROSEBUSH
Population Problems in Nashville, Tennessee   J. PAUL MCCONNELL

Decision of Character (Reprint)   JOHN FOSTER
God in These Times   HENRY P. VAN DUSEN

    * In preparation.

OTHER BOOKS

BY HENRY P. VAN DUSEN

THE PLAIN MAN SEEKS FOR GOD

IN QUEST OF LIFE'S MEANING

VENTURES IN BELIEF
CHRISTIAN CONVICTIONS FOR A DAY OF UNCERTAINTY
A SYMPOSIUM EDITED BY HENRY P. VAN DUSEN

THE STORY OF JESUS
(WITH THOMAS W. GRAHAM)

GOD IN THESE TIMES

God in These Times

By

Henry P. Van Dusen

*Associate Professor of Systematic Theology
and the Philosophy of Religion,
Union Theological Seminary, New York City*

"Have ye not known? have ye not heard?
Hath it not been told you from the beginning?
It is he that sitteth above the circle of the earth,
And the inhabitants thereof are as grasshoppers.
All the nations are as nothing before him;
They are accounted by him as nothing, and vanity."

CHARLES SCRIBNER'S SONS
NEW YORK - - LONDON
1935

NOTE

*While this book was in preparation, the author was asked to con-
tribute an essay, "The Mood of Our Generation," to the symposium, "The Christian Message and the World Today" (A.
L. Warnshuis, Editor). That essay has been incorporated in
Chapter One through the courtesy of the Round Table Press.*

TO

THE MEMBERS OF

THE COMMISSION ON CHRISTIAN FAITH AND LIFE
OF THE WORLD'S STUDENT CHRISTIAN FEDERATION
AND
THE THEOLOGICAL DISCUSSION GROUP

PREFACE

The title of this book suggests a double meaning. That is deliberate. Its purpose is two-fold—to define the place conceded to God in the life and thought of these times, *and* to discover the influence he is actually exerting in men's affairs today. In the contrast between that definition and that discovery is the theme of the book. In that contrast also, in the author's opinion, is to be found the key to the religious problem of our day.

These chapters may be regarded as a sequel to an earlier book, *The Plain Man Seeks for God*. There it was suggested that the sickness of contemporary religion may be traced to two main sources—the dominant intellectual outlook of the past century and a half, and the actual character of modern life—and that, of these, the second is probably the more important. But attention then was directed almost entirely to the intellectual problem. The main concern of the present book is to discover what has been transpiring in the life of the modern world which has so vitally affected the influence and message of religion. It makes no claim to restate the Christian message for today. The author is quite incompetent for such an undertaking, even if it were clear that the time is fully ripe. Rather, its purpose is to urge the imperative need for fundamental rethinking, and then to propose certain preliminary considerations which must guide restatement in two important areas—the Christian message concerning God and the Christian message for society's life. The book closes with a discussion of two particularly pressing concrete questions.

Much of the material was originally prepared for delivery as the annual lectures at the Y. M. C. A. Graduate School, Nashville, Tenn. But those who heard the lectures will hardly recognize them here; the material has been recast, greatly expanded and entirely rewritten. To the officers, staff, and students of the three schools of religion in Nashville who joined as hosts on that occasion, I am indebted for gracious hospitality and encouragement. Thanks are also due Professor John C. Bennett of Auburn Theological Seminary who criticized a preliminary draft of the manuscript; and to Miss Lydia B. Miller for her help in preparing it for the press.

I have taken the liberty of dedicating these essays to the members of two groups—one international, one American—who are seeking to discover the Christian message for our time, and with whom it is my privilege to be associated.

H. P. V. D.

New York, N. Y.
  May 23, 1935.

CONTENTS

CONTENTS

CHAPTER ONE

THE MESSAGE AND THE MAN OF TODAY

Two initial recognitions must guide any one who would deal intelligently with problems of thought at a particular moment of history. *First,* the most important popular assumptions and convictions at any time tend to be determined by the life of that time, by what is actually transpiring in the experience of those who hold them. *Second,* popular thought tends to change by a continuous process of action and reaction—often from one extreme to its opposite.

These generalizations characterize human thought everywhere and in all times. They are especially true of America. Probably more than anywhere else in the world, with us action precedes thought; practice dictates principle; what men do determines what they believe. As for the second—the sharp pendulum-swings of conviction—what more convincing illustration than the story of Prohibition? Or, before that, the reversal of national attitude toward the League of Nations and our international responsibilities? Any American who is determined to understand his country at whatever sacrifice of national pride must accept this as one of our deepest, most ineradicable and most revealing char-

3

acteristics as a people—the inveterate tendency to gulp entire some enthusiasm or conviction under the dictation of impulse or passing wind of doctrine; and then later to vomit it up, completely undigested, and rush to swallow its extreme opposite. To change the figure, we are the intellectual chameleons of the human race.

It is the first of these recognitions which must direct us in this chapter. We are to seek the explanation of the prevailing popular mood in the dominant features of the general life of our time.

I

The man of today is a child of the Modern Age. He has been born into a world preformed for his advent. He has been suckled and reared within its life—a home comfortably appointed for his convenience, lavishly responsive to his desires, proudly conscious of his importance, confidently expectant of his future. As youth has matured and he has taken on manhood, he has been permitted to taste of its pleasures, to discover its convictions, to be initiated into its assumptions, its ambitions, its standards, its hopes. He has found them all good. Thus, they have become organically ingrafted within his own life—part and parcel of his inmost being. Today he is a faithful reflection of the times which have given him birth.

4

It need hardly be pointed out that to his blood parents he has not always responded so uncritically. Maturing experiences have suggested comparison with other and better parents than his; modern psychology has illumined the handicaps which early conditioning has laid upon him; he has reflected upon the devastating contrast between his upbringing and that which he intends for his own children. He has been unable to stifle righteous resentment against his inadequate rearing. The result is the familiar hiatus between the older and younger generations.

But from his social parentage he has experienced no such alienation. For one thing, the instruments of criticism are not his. There *is* no alternative parentage which might suggest unfavorable comparison. He knows nothing of history; therefore he has no calculus for judgment between his own heritage and that of earlier generations. Moreover, he finds his world exceedingly comfortable, exciting, eminently satisfactory; there is no inner stimulus to criticism. If, in recent months, a shadow of distrust has crept across his attitude toward his world, it is a very late appearance. Not many years ago, some one explaining the contemporary disinterest in an after-life, pictured the saints above peering eagerly over the rim of Heaven to learn the latest news from this thrilling, alluring scene below, like stay-at-home fans crowded around the radio in the final minutes of a championship game. Whatever

Heaven might be like, it must be deadly dull in comparison with Twentieth Century America. We all knew his picture was sound. For the most part the man of today has been not only a faithful reflection of the Modern Age but also its grateful and ardent eulogist.

II

In the advance of what we call 'the Modern Age,' three parallel phases may be clearly distinguished. To be sure, they developed simultaneously, acting and reacting upon one another continuously. They appear as three aspects of a single movement; but their discrimination aids a clearer understanding of the modern scene. We may speak of them as *Modern Life, Modern Thought,* and the *Modern Mood. Modern Life* embraces the objective setting of the age—the more obvious and external circumstances of the life of all children of the time—the events which captured men's interest and registered their history, the concerns which claimed their devotion and furnished their satisfactions. By *Modern Thought* we mean the consciously developed philosophies of the period—developed and prized largely by the small company of the intelligentsia (and, incidentally, never as influential as they suppose). For it has not been the articulate philosophies of the schools, but factors far more subtle and undefined

6

which, all through these recent years, have been determining the attitudes of the common man—the half-understood feelings and half-articulated convictions and half-recognized assumptions which are his philosophy of life. These, it is, which constitute what we call the *Modern Mood*. This is the major object of our interest. But a hasty glance at its two companion factors will prepare the way for a clearer grasp of the mood of today. And, first, *Modern Life*.

III

To interpret the life of any period in terms of a single influence is to be guilty of over-simplification. But few would question that there is one pre-eminently important key to the development of the world's life in the past century—*the advance of man's effective mastery over Nature*.

The tale is too familiar, too threadbare, to permit retelling again. We sicken of the reiterated statistics, the incomprehensible comparisons; our fatigued imaginations refuse to stir to a fresh grasping of it all. The facts remain none the less. They were given graphic and final portraiture in the recent Century of Progress Exposition in Chicago. Whether we regard it as the supreme expression of man's consummate genius, or as a pathetic proof of modern man's preoccupation with the mechanical and the tawdry, the truth of history

7

which the Exposition demonstrated is beyond dispute. The life of every one of us in any age is compact of two great sets of factors. The one, the external circumstances of life, differs from age to age and marks each man's and each generation's distinctive history. The other, the primordial forces within his own soul and the problems they beget, each man largely shares with all mankind; they vary little from age to age. Of the two great factors which determine man's experience, one—the first—has suffered more radical transformation within the lifetime of our generation than in all of human history before. The external setting of the life of every citizen of the western world today —all that surrounds his spirit and makes incessant impact upon it, moulding and fashioning it beyond his realization—is more completely different from that of his grandfather than his grandfather's was from that of Socrates. It is a new creation. That fact furnishes the key to *Modern Life*.

The by-products of this basic fact are likewise a tale too familiar. Let us mention four:

1. The advance of man's effective mastery over Nature has accomplished the unification of the world. Through multiplied and instant communication, through the world-wide dispersion of invention and education and culture, through interlocking commercial and financial interests, the peoples of the world live in continuous and intimate contact with each

other; and their interests are largely one. *And* this unification has found its most significant expression in —*the World War.*

2. The advance of man's effective mastery over Nature has, for the first time in all human history, made thoroughly practicable the provision of adequate food, shelter, security, education, recreation and a modest comfort for every single inhabitant of the western world. *And* that possibility has taken actuality in—*the present Depression,* with its immeasurable want, hardship, degradation and despair.

3. The advance of man's effective mastery over Nature has opened wide the doorway to culture, acquaintance with the rich treasures of man's past, participation in the delicate and deep imponderables of the human spirit for all who will enter. *And* the most general response to that invitation has been—the movies, the radio, jazz.

4. The advance of man's effective mastery over Nature has promised modern man achievements and satisfactions beyond the wildest dreams of his forbears. *And* that promise has seen realization in the typical successful American of today—superficial, crude, blatant, confused, restless, inwardly dissatisfied.

The promise—a united world, security and comfort, culture, happiness. The fulfillment—a World War, the Depression, jazz, disillusionment. A partial and one-sided picture, to be sure; one thread among many.

But will any one question that it is the dominant character of the portrait of our world's life today, the central thread in the tangled skein which is *Modern Life?*

IV

What of the consciously formulated philosophies of the age—the structure of *Modern Thought?*

Here, also, amidst the currents and eddies of intellectual controversy in the past century, it is impossible to miss one single major key to the development. One problem, thrusting itself into prominence early in the century and gaining centrality as the modern movement advanced, has furnished the setting, determined the issues and in large measure dictated the terms of philosophic discussion—the relation of science to traditional tenets. The great preoccupation of modern thought has been to agree upon the meaning of science for our general world outlook. The main issues of debate have sprung from seeming conflicts between the implications of science and generally accepted assumptions. The newer schools, consolidating an ever firmer leadership, have made their aim the complete and final displacement of older views by a 'scientific philosophy.' Science has dictated the terms of the modern intellectual quest.

The results of this ascendancy of a scientific outlook

and methodology are easily defined. Inevitably, it focused the attention of thought upon those aspects of reality and of human experience with which science was prepared most readily to deal to the neglect or denial of other aspects which eluded scientific categories. That meant a concentration upon the general rather than the individual, the primitive rather than the mature, the uniform rather than the unique, the familiar rather than the original, the quantitative rather than the qualitative, the commonplace rather than the delicate, the rare, the meaningful, the profound. In brief, it fostered and glorified a perspective directly antipodal to that which the nobler philosophies had made their own; and a preoccupation with data at precisely the opposite pole from that which these philosophies had learned to recognize as most significant.

However, it was not only the intellectual principles and conclusions of science which were vitally determining the development of *Modern Thought*. Even more important was *the character of world-life* which science was making possible and with the actual erection of which it was tirelessly busied. Ideally it is philosophy's distinctive function to criticize the culture of its day in the light of higher and truer perspectives. In reality, it rises to that high vocation but rarely. More frequently, it takes its cue from prevailing popular enthusiasms instead of from the wealth of its historic treasures. The outcome of its labors is not the correction of prevailing assumptions by the touchstone of wider truths, but a rationalization of those assumptions into intellectual respectability. Thought becomes the servile handmaiden of that to which it should be relentless tutor.

This is, very largely, the story of philosophy in the past century. It is, I hope, not unfair to the regnant schools to suggest that their subconscious and probably controlling motivation was to develop a view of things which should be thoroughly harmonious with the dominant temper of *Modern Life*. Not so much consistency with scientific theory (though that was important) as congruity with contemporary life was the chief concern. Like the man in the street, the philosopher found his world good; he yearned to outfit it with respectable and impressive intellectual dress. So we see philosophy throughout the period scuffling in confused and undignified haste to effect a tardy adjustment to the interests, desires and presuppositions of the life of the day. *Modern Life* was intensely absorbed in the techniques and externals and appurtenances of living (bathtubs, motor-cars, aeroplanes, electric refrigeration, radios), relatively oblivious to its delicate and personal inner apprehensions; so *Thought* became. *Modern Life* found its great ally and servant in technical science and, like the lion in John Masefield's *Son of Adam*, was quickly imprisoned within science's skillfully wrought mechanisms; *Thought* followed suit and suffered like imprisonment. *Modern Life* fastened men's admiring attention upon their own abilities, encouraging in them a quite exaggerated sense of importance and security; *Modern Thought* translated this habitual attitude into a self-conscious theory of reality. In brief, the philosophies most characteristic of the time became increasingly pallid and rather pitiable mirrorings of the society in which they dwelt—naturalistic, materialistic, humanistic, pragmatistic, and above all, supine and servile. In wide circles, thought gave over its responsibility of criticism and correction for the easier if somewhat ludicrous rôle of accommodation and imitation.

V

From the point of view of our special interest—religion's status in the life of today—one comment must be interjected. The more recent tendencies must not be taken too seriously. A longer perspective is demanded. In that perspective, it is clear that scientific thought and scientific civilization have not created the problem; they have accentuated it and given it the particular form in which contemporary man sees it. With all of the revolutionary developments of the nineteenth century, the situation of Christianity—both its intellectual respectability and its popular effectiveness—was not greatly different at the close of the century than at its beginning. Indeed, the parallel between the two century-turns is arresting. It has been pointed out that the eighteenth century left religion "apparently helpless in the face of the rationalistic attack." To recall the plight of the church at that period is almost to imagine one is viewing the situation of the church today.[1] It was a temporary discomfiture, however. So extreme a scepticism and indifference as that which dominated the close of the eighteenth century bred inevitable reaction. Through the united impact of the Wesleyan revival, the Romantic movement, and the rehabilitation of intuition and faith, religion experienced a recovery of confidence in message and power in society. Our grandfathers dwelt in an 'age of faith.' Only later came the impact of modern science as we know it. Then the history of the preceding century was repeated in almost identical terms.

The point is that the tension in which Christian thought finds itself in our time is not solely a feature of the scientific age. It has been characteristic of the past three centuries rather than of the last century alone. It springs from conflict between the Christian view of man and the world and another view which long antedated modern science but which has hailed the 'scientific viewpoint' as a ready ally. And the issues of that tension, while they present themselves to the

[1] See, for example, John Buchan, *Sir Walter Scott*, Chap. I. *Cf.* John Herman Randall, Jr., *The Making of the Modern Mind*, p. 519.

14

man of today in the particular dress determined by scientific thought, are essentially the same—a philosophy based upon selective abstraction *or* a philosophy seeking to encompass *all* of reality with its fathomless depth and richness and variety; the search for truth with the processes of logical inductive reason alone, *or* with every faculty of the human spirit; the assertion of man's centrality in creation and unbounded confidence in man's powers both to know and to do, *or* the recognition of man's finiteness before the majesty and mystery of the Universe in which his lot is cast and a humble confession of man's limited powers to know and his tragically faltering willingness to do the right.

VI

In such a setting of world-life and thought-world we discover the man of today. They have bred and nurtured him. What shall we say of him, and of his convictions, his assumptions, his hopes, his misgivings —all that constitutes the *Modern Mood?*

The main meaning of what has gone before is clear enough. Like the plain man of any age, the convictions of the man of today have been taken up bodily out of the life of the times into which he happens to have been born. His most secure premises are, in overwhelming majority, uncriticized reflections of the prevailing interests and hopes of his society. Three major influences the Modern Age has had upon his attitudes and his feelings for life. It has severed his living connection with the past; it has fastened his hopes in the machine; it has fostered a consciousness of unprecedented human autonomy and power.

Not only has the temper of the age encouraged a disdain of tradition and the riches of history; for the average man it has actually severed a vital connection with the past. A few years ago a well-known professor of psychology was fond of telling his students that he could not understand why any one should recommend a text-book in any subject written more than fifteen years previously—the year in which he first began to teach behavioristic psychology. That is an absurd exaggeration of the dominant attitude of the *Modern Mood*. Poor deluded mortal! If only he could be persuaded to turn the pages of the history he so despises, he would see his prototype in 400 B.C., again in the age of Augustus, in 350 A.D., at the Renaissance, in the middle of the eighteenth century—each man equally supercilious toward the past, equally certain that knowledge would henceforth be dated from his age. He would see, also, the long sweeping tides of time carry his prototypes away and make of them and their epochs but flickering specks in the ebb and flow of man's age-long search for truth.

As we have said, the man of today knows no history;

he has been led to think history unimportant. He knows nothing of the underlying corporate psychological forces which so largely determine any age and those who inhabit it. He has no comprehension of the great cyclic movements of action and reaction in man's thought and man's progress which determine that periods of soaring idealism are succeeded by times of blunt realism; that romanticism and emotionalism and optimism make way for conservatism, dogmatism, reaction; that sophistication is usually followed by moral sterility; that high prosperity gives birth to superficiality, then arrogance, then profligacy, then disillusionment, then disgust with the world, then cynicism, then moral decline, and finally disintegration and retrogression. He lacks the first mark of education and the prerequisite to culture—historic perspective. Therefore he has no equipment, if he desired it, to locate the significance of his own day in the drama of history and, thereby, to judge and correct his own instinctive assumptions. In brief, he has no real understanding of the times in which he lives. By the same token, he possesses no valid vision for the future, no grasp of the course ahead which progress must take, if there is to be progress. And no commanding passion that the stuff of this present shall be moulded into the possibilities of that visioned future.

In similar fashion, he is spiritually impoverished, divorced from the sources of a significant culture. We have thought to build a culture out of modern life. But, even if the materials for the enhancement of culture were present (and that is by no means certain), one cannot build a culture over night, one cannot build a culture *de novo,* one cannot build a culture out of machinery and household conveniences, one cannot *build* a culture at all. It must grow. It must grow from soil rich and fallow for its nurture, by the slow processes of natural development and enrichment. In American life there were seedplots from which a sound and significant culture might have flowered. The early American tradition, especially in New England and the old South, was fertile in rootage for a national culture. Indeed it had given unmistakable promise for the future by a preliminary flowering in the 'Golden Day' of American literature and art. And there were other hopeful seedplots, in the frontier tradition and elsewhere. But the whole impact of modern life has tended to cut connection with that tradition, to breed disdain of it and its possible gifts for life, to relegate all pre-machine-age achievements to the museum of antiquities, and to advertise the 'new culture' which science and the machine and modern man together would construct.

So the man in the street stands today, rootless—a prodigious, overgrown, adolescent sapling—swayed by every wind of doctrine, without the rootage which might have furnished him with security and stability against the blizzards and devastating simoons of the times and without the deep satisfactions which are possible to firmly founded men in any age.

Again, the Modern Age has fastened his hopes in the machine. As I have elsewhere suggested, 'It has fixed his attention upon the amassing of things, the multiplication of accoutrements, the perfecting of appliances and contrivances. It has persuaded him that plumbing is more important than poetry, facts than understanding, the latest than the best, standardization than individuality, quantity output than originality, success than life.' It was significant that, with all the hue and cry over 'Technocracy,' almost no one raised question at its fundamental premise—that, since machinery can steadily increase output with diminishing human labor, there will be less and less work for men to do. But machinery cannot paint a Sistine Madonna; machinery cannot produce handcraft; machinery cannot erect a Chartres Cathedral, as many of our contemporary churches abundantly testify. It is obvious that machinery is powerless to supply to the life of man any gift where worth attaches to richness and depth, to originality and subtlety and individuality. It is powerless to furnish channels through which all that is most delicate and personal and profound in human aspiration and insight might find expression. It is some measure of the spiritual reality and fertility of the

Modern Mood that it contemplated with confident sat-
isfaction a machine-made civilization.

Finally, the Modern Age has fostered in its children
a consciousness of unprecedented human autonomy
and almost unlimited power. This was the inevitable
result of its influence at every point. By creating a new
world of outward circumstance, it suggested that a new
order of men had appeared as authors and sovereigns
of that world. By providing tools of size and speed and
power, it imputed vicarious greatness and strength to
those who wield them. By enclosing men within the
satisfactions of their machine-dominated life and away
from Nature's immensities and mysteries, it foreshort-
ened perspective and fostered a grotesque self-impor-
tance. By severing contact with the riches of earlier
human achievement, it prevented comparisons which
might have induced more intelligent humility. By
magnifying genuine accomplishments in a single aspect
of experience, it encouraged the impression of mastery
over every problem. By fastening an intent attention
upon step by step advance in the chosen path, it created
the illusion of general progress and blinded men to the
precipices inevitably ahead. Nothing seemed able so
much as to joggle man's unbridled self-confidence—
not the War, the most gigantic corporate folly in all
human history; nor even the Depression, direct fruit
of the most blatant stupidity and greed in civilized

times. Modern man "burns incense to himself and his own countenance is veiled from him in the smoke."[2]

These are the outward features of the *Modern Mood*. Nevertheless, to describe them only is to give a quite false impression of the deeper and hidden temper of that *Mood*. We have already suggested that one of the most characteristic expressions of the age was jazz. Would any one who has moved freely in the midstream of life through these recent years question it? But what is jazz?

"Jazz is the perfect symbol of our mood: raucous ribaldry on the surface, with a deep undercurrent of the blues, syncopated to conceal the heartbreak, blaring loud dissonant defiance at all who would presume to question the genuineness of its hilarity."[3]

And the bearer of that mood, the typical man of today —"that strange, absurd, pathetic, notable, conquering Hamlet of the modern world, with his catchwords and his motor-cars, a score of platitudes on his lips and a score of unrealized desires in his heart."[4]

Beneath the thin veneer of satisfied self-assurance, the man of today is a strangely bewildered, frustrated, profoundly unhappy mortal.

[2] C. G. Jung, *Modern Man in Search of a Soul*, p. 246.
[3] Walter M. Horton, *Theism and the Modern Mood*, p. 7.
[4] Struthers Burt.

VII

But that is not the final word.

If our description truly portrays the life and mood of today, or even of yesterday, it is a day which, in tomorrow's view, will seem a dead and distant past. The *Modern Mood* with all its baggage of presuppositions and pretensions is disappearing under our eyes. It is disappearing under a twofold influence—disintegration within and devastating attack from without.

A few years ago, visitors from abroad reported that in Europe men were becoming uncertain in their own autonomy. Then that uncertainty found no echo in American life. Today, we confront a generation shorn of self-confidence—disillusioned of its leadership, disillusioned as to the significance of its own achievement, disillusioned of its ability to save the crumbling remnants of its proud domain. The florid optimism of yesterday has evaporated overnight. A new situation has lowered upon us like a dark and sudden squall on spanking, sparkling wavelets. It demands new equipment and new skills. As a ship, caught unprepared, heaves to clumsily to reef in the teeth of the storm, men are searching their souls to test their adequacy for the demands of a new day.

Our generation knows it has been betrayed. If the betrayal is of its own making, the bitterness is no less on that account. The leadership, the assumptions, the dominant institutions of the Modern Age stand under severe condemnation. A craving for authority is gnawing at men's spirits. Sir Michael Sadler, describing prevailing attitudes among Oxford undergraduates, says: "The young are eager and hungry—for faith, for work, for a leader whom they can trust and follow without question. . . . They are not interested in what at one time I would have gone to the stake for—I mean liberty of thought. Give them the possibility of ardour in achievement and they would not care a hang about —for example—the freedom of the Press. . . . Once the young have found their leader and accepted his purpose, there will be a revolution." [5] There, one suspects, is the mood of tomorrow.

To the facts of internal disintegration must be added the factors of external attack. Across the world today there are forces powerfully at play which are dissolving the *Modern Mood* like cheap amalgam under strong acid. And the acids which are purging and testing the world's life in this hour are far more potent, far more irresistible than the famed 'acids of modernity.' Everywhere there are causes and faiths powerfully clamant for men's allegiance. They bear not the slightest resemblance to the attitudes and movements which have been alluring the man of today throughout the modern period. In every corner of the

[5] *Have We Lost God?* ed. by W. R. Titterton, pp. 19–21.

world, two such faiths are foremost—nationalism and communism. They do not invite participation; they command allegiance. They do not persuade to hypotheses; they declare finalities. They do not encourage discussion; they silence criticism. They do not promise satisfactions; they demand sacrifice. They do not pamper men; they conscript their very souls. They do not magnify the individual; they require his all in the service of the whole. But from that complete self-giving they propose to build a new world for all mankind.

These are the forces which press their commands upon the man of today. His mind, lulled by the comforting self-inflation and easy-going agnosticisms of the Modern Age, is ill-tempered for the challenge of their confident dogmatisms. His life, made flabby in the lush worldliness of modern life, is ill-prepared for the rigor of their disciplines. In the face of these dogmatic and demanding causes, weak men stand vacillating in impotent indecision. Strong men—or those who wish to convey the impression of strength—rush to speedy and unthinking enlistment.

The sum of it all is, the incense of self-glorification which modern men have been burning at their own altar is speedily evaporating. We begin to see ourselves truly at last. And the mirror returns to us a disquietingly stupid and flabby and bewildered countenance. Ours is the paralysis of humiliating self-discovery.

VIII

The relevance of all we have been saying for our concern should be patent. It is to the man of today— a child of the Modern Age, bitterly disillusioned of his parentage, tragically ill-equipped for the rigors of the new day, baffled and nerveless before the onset of the currents of the times—it is to him that the Christian faith must bring its message.

What are the implications for that message? Two, I would suggest. First a word of warning. If it is the tendency of human thought (and especially in this land) to move by sharp pendulum-swings from one exaggerated extreme to its opposite, then Christianity must anticipate just such a sharp reaction from the whole viewpoint of the modern temper and must seek to moderate it in the service of the larger truth. For Christianity's only allegiance is to TRUTH—not half-truth or part-truth, of whatever complexion.

Second and much more important. In the measure that it has been an organic part, a servile and faithful representative, of an age which stands under severe condemnation and is passing away under our eyes, the Christian message must shake itself loose from its present entanglements; and must bring not only the life of today but its own thought and life under the judgment of the most rigorous and unsparing re-examination. Positively, it must search afresh for its own distinctive and true roots and norms. This is to "re-think its message." With two aspects of that enterprise, we shall attempt to deal further—its thought of God, and its critique of existing society.

CHAPTER TWO

THE MESSAGE OF THE LIVING GOD

CHAPTER TWO

THE MESSAGE OF THE LIVING GOD

SOMETHING is wrong with men's faith in God today. On that fact I suppose we should all be agreed. Not mainly the faith of those who are professional religious leaders, but the working, effective faith of the great body of ordinary folk—those who make up the rank and file of our population, and of our churches.

To be sure, it is quite possible to exaggerate the gravity of the contemporary sickness of religion. Sometimes it appears that what is most needed is that the churches should give over brooding upon their ills, cease from spiritual self-diagnosis, assume normality, and get down to the business of living confidently and healthily. Nevertheless, where there is so much pain, there must be infection; where there is so much talk, there must be solid reason for it. Something is fundamentally wrong with men's living faith in God today.

The previous chapter sought to picture the development of secular thought and life in recent decades. We must now bring the more general analysis to focus upon religion. What is it that has been happening to religious faith during the Modern Age? Our purpose in this chapter is two-fold—to search out the basic causes of the present situation, and to propose a sounder approach in the whole matter.

I

If our initial premise is correct—that men's working convictions tend to take their color from the character of the society in which they dwell—we should expect to discover the secret of the illness of contemporary faith in God in the life of the Modern Age itself. We are not mistaken.

Generally speaking, the religion of today is a typical and wholly loyal child of that Age—bone of its bone and flesh of its flesh. The interpretation of the last chapter concerned secular life and thought. At every important point, religion has shared fully the distinguishing features there described. To a sensitive and candid churchman, the portrayal of these times is self-portraiture.[1] This is equally true of the churches' thought and of their life.

The life of the church has drunk deep of the enthusiasms of the secular world and fallen heavily under

[1] Professor Paul Tillich points out that the factors which most powerfully determined spiritual developments during the modern period may be most readily detected, not in the specifically religious field, but in the great areas of secular concern—in art, literature, science, politics, and common life. By the same token, the reaction against the spiritual betrayal of the Modern Age which is such a vivid feature of the present day appeared first in secular areas. (See his brilliant exposition in *The Religious Situation,* tr. by H. R. Niebuhr.) This is further indication of the servility of formal religion to the temper of the times.

the spell of its assumptions and its ideals. Bigger and grander churches, more and cleverer mechanical contrivances, larger and more inflated budgets, sermon-topics inspired by newspaper headlines, sermon-treatment guided by advertising technique, sermon-results tested by external and numerical computation, the aims of the church defined in harmony with prevailing secular goals, the power of the church measured by accepted business norms—in these and many other more subtle ways, the modern church has been fully within the fabric of *Modern Life* and has been jubilantly faithful to its central temper.

And the thought of the churches, their theology? We have pictured secular *Modern Thought* in undignified scramble to 'keep up with the Jones' of *Modern Life*. How could one draw a true portrait of the most advanced Christian thinking in our time except in that posture so familiar to us all—scurrying in precipitate and breathless embarrassment to bring the interpretation of religion into conformity with the latest dogmas of secular thought? Christian apologists these recent years have reminded one painfully of the small-town society leader who brings her young daughter up to the great metropolis of learning and fashion—the same self-revealing haste to re-dress the child in the latest metropolitan mode, with the inevitable result of a rather crude overdressing; the same nervous solicitude lest the child commit an unpardonable *faux pas,* with the inevitable result of painful self-consciousness and artificiality; the same stupid attempt to force spontaneous, eager life into highly artificial and decadent moulds, with the inevitable result not only of insincerity but of violation of the child's true nature. The simile is, perhaps, not wholly unsuggestive. But it requires one important modification. The ward which Christian thinkers have had entrusted to their charge for introduction into the maelstrom of modern thought was no innocent adolescent. It was—the majestic, mature wisdom of the Christian faith, embracing much of the accumulated riches of man's agelong quest for truth, and fated to make its invaluable gifts to modern life only at the hands of the professional apologist. That is the betrayal for which recent Christian thought must do long and prostrate penance.

We have urged that it is the special task of philosophy not to follow but to guide current trends, to correct not obey their assumptions; but that it seldom exercises its rightful function. How much more is it the bounden duty of religion to stand apart from the transient aberrations of the moment and bring them under the judgment of its own higher insights! To fail in that responsibility is to stand without excuse. And it is to ring religion's own deathknell.

The basic perspective of the Modern Age was seriously distorted. Many of its underlying and unquestioned assumptions were quite false, some of them palpably absurd. Inevitably the religion which was so ready a protégé of the Age was infected with its short-comings, its fallacies, its absurdities. Here is the most important single cause of religion's impotence.

II

What, more precisely, were the ways by which the Modern Age was fashioning the present plight of religious faith?

Men are never skillful in diagnosing their own spiritual illness; the most sensitive of them are reasonably acute in sensing its presence. They know that something is rotten in the state of Denmark; they are inept in defining what that something is. For example, in the early years of the last century, the Romantic poets were deeply stirred by antagonism toward the mechanistic point of view which was winning a growing ascendancy. As Whitehead reminds us, they "felt that something had been left out, and that what had been left out comprised everything that was most important." [2] But they were never completely successful in fastening their fingers on the crucial omissions. Similarly, all through the recent era, the wisest men, many of them without speaking acquaintance with technical philosophy or book-learning, knew in their

[2] A. N. Whitehead, *Science and the Modern World*, p. 108.

bones that something very fundamental was lacking in the whole outlook and perspective of the modern mind. Few could explain to themselves or to others where the heart of the trouble lay. In each period, the basic error was the same—the *fallacy of abstraction*.

It is probable that the most serious intellectual and spiritual vice to which the human mind is tempted is that of abstraction. By abstraction, we mean the mistaking of the part for the whole, or the reading of the whole in terms of some fragmentary part. Abstraction is blindness to the 'both—ands' of life.[3] It is the most fecund parent of fallacy, of bigotry, of Pharisaism, of heresy. It is the usual begetter of false and flabby religion.

Scientists concentrate their energies upon one phase or level of Nature's imponderable and inapprehensible richness, achieve some measure of control over that phase or level, and then interpret the whole of Nature in those terms; that was the chief vice of nineteenth-century science. Philosophers reflect upon one aspect of the innumerable paradoxes and antinomies with which Reality confronts us—the inexorability of determinism or the certitude of freedom, the fact of matter or the fact of mind, the high worth of reason or the

---

[3] "An abstraction is nothing else than an omission of part of the truth." A. N. Whitehead, *Nature and Life,* p. 32. This is the intellectual vice to which Whitehead gives the name the 'Fallacy of Misplaced Concreteness.' His *Science and the Modern World* is in large part an exposure of that fallacy and a demonstration of its strangling grip upon the thought of our time.

validity of intuition—and construct their systems upon
that single aspect to the neglect or denial of other and
equally indisputable aspects. Educators are intrigued
by some single theory or branch of knowledge or
period of history, become enamored of its importance,
exaggerate its significance out of all true proportion,
and deny their pupils exposure to other vast areas and
phases and periods of knowledge. Religious folk fasten
upon the distinctive experience and creed which have
brought liberation to their spirits and forthwith pro-
nounce heretical religion which has come to others in
radically different fashion. It will be discovered, I
think, that men go astray in their thought of God
almost always through some error of abstraction. False
ideas of God are partial ideas of God. And partial
ideas of God are never long-lived. Their defects are
exposed and they disappear and give place to no belief
in God at all. Abstraction is the unfailing father of
atheism.

Now the thought and life of the past half century
have been literally riddled with abstractions. They
were implicit in almost every feature of the temper of
the times—its lust for analysis, its passion for specialization, its preoccupation with the here and now, its
artificial capitalist economy, its mechanized personal
and social life, its haughty egoism, its overweening self-
sufficiency. In the realm of research, each of the particular sciences has isolated its own selected material

in abstraction from the data of other sciences and from the more general cosmic nexus which is its conditioning environment—often with serious distortion in conclusions. Contemporary science is in vigorous reaction from such abstraction. In the world of learning, specialization has isolated particular topics in abstraction from their organic setting—blinding men to the larger whole and unfitting them to seek or to recognize general meanings. "The increasing departmentalization of universities during the last hundred years, however necessary for administrative purposes, tends to trivialize the mentality of the teaching profession." [4] In the arena of business, the pace and practice of the prevailing system have isolated each operator in abstraction not merely from the larger horizons of the corporate fabric but from the richer goods of life—dulling him to the meaning of his own existence. In industry, the mechanism of production has riveted each workman to his machine in abstraction from the organic process—strangling the creative craftsmanship which is the essence and redemptive principle of all true labor. In the common life, the whole exultant bravado of the times has isolated modern man in abstraction from history, from Nature, from culture, from beauty, from profound comradeship, from the mysterious profundities of his own soul.

The omnipresence of abstractions was perhaps the

[4] A. N. Whitehead, *Nature and Life*, p. 16.

most marked feature of the age.[5] Three, in particular,
have exerted a determining influence upon the adequacy and the vitality of men's thought about God.
They have insinuated themselves into the working assumptions of the man of today so gradually, so im-
perceptibly, that for the most part he is quite unaware
of their presence. Only a deliberate and painful effort
of self-analysis is likely to reveal them and their devastating power over him. One, to which we have just
alluded, is the divorce in scientific procedure of its distinctive subject-matter from the larger whole of Reality, and the restriction of the legitimate material for
religious belief to the data and conclusions of science.
In brief it is the modern mind's insistence upon a so-
called 'scientific theology.' The second is the divorce
in religious thought between the realm of private life
and the realm of public life, and the careful confine-
ment of God's activity to the former. More simply, it
is the modern man's severance in his practical religion
of personal piety from public practice, and the tacit
denial of God's reign in society. The third is the divorce in popular thought of man himself from the
cosmos which is his Begetter, his Sustainer, and the

[5] I have not delayed to labor this point. But its recognition is absolutely
fundamental to the argument of this book. Some of the more patent instances of abstraction in the life of the man of today have appeared in Chap.
I or will be pointed out below. The pervasion of recent thought and life
by abstraction has been described in detail in the writings of Professor
Whitehead already referred to. This pervasion, together with the current
vigorous reaction in every field of learning and art, has been lucidly por-
trayed by Professor Paul Tillich in *The Religious Situation*.

inexorable Sovereign of his affairs. It is the absurdity of the modern mind's ego-centric perspective.

Fundamental causes of the failing health of contemporary religion are, then, at least three—religion's servile acceptance of 'scientific' norms and methods in its apprehension of Reality; religion's acquiescence in the insincere divorce of public ethics from private profession; religion's docile adoption of a man-centred perspective. It is the second of these which has been most intimately involved in the fabric of the modern man's religion; it is this which must claim our major attention. However, we may well pause for brief notice of the complementary and more theoretical influence— that of the scientific outlook.

III

Religion has followed modern thought in looking to science for instructions in the development and defense of its convictions. Among intelligent people, especially in more advanced circles, the impression has increasingly gained hold that religious belief is valid—and those who hold it intellectually respectable—only in so far as it has passed the most exacting scientific tests; many would feel only in the measure that it is directly derived from the conclusions of the particular sciences. The aim has been a 'scientific theology.' Let it be noted, in passing, that when men speak of a 'scientific theology,' they may mean one of two quite different things—either the erection of a quite new structure of beliefs from materials supplied exclusively by the sciences themselves, discarding all other possible material not so derived; or the reconstruction of theology from both old and new materials by employment of a *method* which science prescribes, the so-called 'scientific method.' In whichever meaning, whether science was expected to furnish both materials and method or method only, science was prescribing the conditions for the formulation of a valid theology.

The whole problem of the relations of science and theology, as old as modern thought itself and painfully hackneyed by now, is too vast and too complex to be considered here. Moreover, we are not concerned with every aspect of the influence of science upon religion, but only with the ways in which, as it touched the thought of the average man, it has affected his convictions about God. Lest there be any misunderstanding of our attitude as we approach the matter, let it be said at once that I have no sympathy whatever with the pitiable decrying of modern science which has characterized so much religious apologetic in our time. It has been very largely misguided and futile because it wholly misconceived the real issues. If the dominance of theology by scientific influences has been unfortunate, it is for reasons quite different from those advanced by the all too familiar defenders of religion against the 'inroads' of science. Men of intelligence will trust science fully as it goes about its task of discovery and formulation, and will welcome heartily every one of its accredited findings. Indeed, I should want to go a long step farther and affirm that, for me personally and for some years past, the most convincing indications of the reality of God have come directly from the findings of science, and nowhere else. Science does not lead us to all we need to know about God; but it does seem to me to establish his existence by indisputably objective evidence, quite independent of our wishes in the matter, our feelings and our hopes, or even of the testimony of religious experience. That is precisely the kind of evidence we stand in need of if our certainty of God is to be held steady and secure and true.[6]

Why, then, do we list theology's servitude to science as one of the principal causes of the loss of vital faith in God in our time? If the most authoritative conclusions of science are not inimical to religion, how is it that the impact of science has tended to weaken men's hold on God? In two ways. First, because it is increasingly assumed that science is our *sole* guide to truth, that the scientific method is the *only* way by which reality in any form can be apprehended and interpreted by man, and, consequently, that it is the *whole* of

[6] See the author's *The Plain Man Seeks for God,* Chap. III and pp. 109–110.

Reality which science grasps. Secondly, although the *conclusions* of science have increasingly substantiated the religious man's convictions about God, the *habit of mind* which science induces may progressively unfit him for the personal apprehension of God. In the measure that the 'scientific attitude' becomes one's habitual and only approach to reality, to that degree one's sense of the reality of God is likely to become dim, vague, insecure, of little moment.

And for these very good reasons. Science, of avowed purpose, deals with reality of only certain specifications and in only a certain fashion. That is to say, it deals with reality *abstractly*. Inevitably, its account of reality can never be complete or, in itself, wholly adequate; it is an 'abstraction.' Put otherwise, science deliberately assumes a perspective which is partial. Therefore, an interpretation of reality from that perspective must of necessity be partial and in some measure distorted. Likewise, a mind habituated to the perspective of science will never glimpse more than fragments of reality, incomplete and misleading by themselves; it is likely to miss Reality itself altogether. Here is the crux of the matter—not in the accredited findings of scientific inquiry, but in the assumption that they are *all* man knows of reality *and* in the ingrained temper of mind which the 'scientific attitude' begets.

More specifically, what does the scientific mind do in its approach to reality which renders its account inadequate and itself incapable of apprehending the very reality with which it seeks to deal? Let us speak of three things. Two have received passing mention in our discussion of the Modern Age. We may restate them here.[7]

1. Science encourages us to deal with parts, with fragments. Indeed, by virtue of its chosen method of analysis, description, classification and generalization, science must divide its material into the smallest possible units for purposes of treatment. Science is embarrassed before the unique; science is impotent before the whole. But—if there be a God at all, it is quite obvious that he must be the most concrete, the most unique, of all realities. And he must be the most inclusive of all realities, in some sense a WHOLE to which all else is related as parts. Small wonder then that minds trained to think only scientifically and employing exclusively scientific procedures should miss God altogether. They would be very likely, so to speak, to 'pass God by' without ever becoming conscious of him, simply because the meshes of their intellectual apparatus are adjusted to catch objects at the opposite pole from what, if he is at all, he must of necessity be.

2. Again, as we said earlier, science concentrates attention upon the simple rather than the complex, the elementary rather than the advanced, the primitive

---

[7] A different and somewhat fuller analysis of the influence of modern science on religious thought will be found in *The Plain Man Seeks for God*, pp. 55–64.

rather than the mature, the commonplace rather than the delicate, the rare, the meaningful, the profound. But here, likewise, is an instrument ill-fitted to lay hold on God. For, if he is at all, he must be the most delicate, the most complex, the most meaningful of all realities, the absolutely unique Reality. Now we see more clearly why modern religious thought, employing the magnifying glass of scientific method, has so often missed the living God altogether.

3. However, there is a more fundamental and serious disservice of the scientific attitude. It is of the utmost importance that we make it clear to ourselves.

Science deals only with 'objects.' It regards whatever it handles as an individual unit of reality, standing over against it, passively awaiting the advance of its penetrating scrutiny. In the same way it has encouraged men to think of God as an 'object,' one object among other objects, a passive object awaiting man's discovery, analysis and definition. It has thought of God as an 'It' among other 'its.'

Note carefully what happens if we employ this approach in our attitude toward a fellow human being. To attempt so to think of any one is to try to hold his living, pulsating, ever-changing self—all that makes him a significant person and not a mummy—within a straight-jacket of analytic scrutiny. Of course, it cannot be done. The person cannot be so held. Since he refuses to 'stay put,' we find ourselves scrutinizing parts of him, such parts as can be held passive and life-less for our observation. They are, inevitably, the least significant elements in his make-up. In other words, to handle a person after this fashion is no longer to deal with the whole of him, but only with fragments; that is, it is no longer to deal with *him* at all. So to regard any one is to destroy him in the attempt to understand him; and we conclude by not understanding him at all. We complete our analysis and we deliver our verdict. Lo and behold, we no longer have the person in our hands but only his clothing or, it may be, his corpse.

In brief, if you were consistently and persistently to treat me for the space of half a day as an 'object,' an 'it' among other 'its'—so always to think of me and so to speak to me, it is obvious that you would never come into real contact with me. You would never discover anything significant about me. Much more important, the whole relationship would become intolerable be-fore half the appointed time had elapsed. One is re-minded of Clutton-Brock's familiar saying that the man who treated his wife scientifically, that is as one of a class of wives, would never know anything about marriage, or about anything else worth knowing.

If all of this be obvious in our relations with another human being, how immeasurably truer of our appre-hension of God. This is one of the great insights of con-temporary Continental thinkers, a sound note in their protest. If there be a God at all, he must be the most living, vital, active, complex of all realities. He cannot possibly be known as an 'it,' much less as one 'it' among other 'its.' So to think of him is to think of him absolutely incorrectly. As the Europeans are fond of putting it, is not to think of *God* at all. That is, quite literally, true. When you assume such a perspective, that on which you are concentrating is NOT God. It is a lifeless, mummified man-constructed abstraction of the living Reality. Positively, God, if properly thought of, must always and unfailingly be addressed and regarded as the great THOU.

After the same fashion, the search for God which assumes him to be a distant and impassive object toward which our minds must feel their way by tedious and difficult intellectual inquiry will never find him. It does not reach him because it does not know the only possible way to make sure of the Goal of its desire. For, if there be a God at all, he must be an ever-present, all-encompassing Reality who gives to our seeking minds such reality as they possess—One who surrounds and sustains human life, making insistent and never-wearied impact upon it. Only if it be acknowledged that so he *must* be, can he ever be discovered and known.

IV

We turn, now, to that one of the innumerable abstractions characteristic of the modern outlook which bears most powerfully upon our central interest—religion's acquiescence in the modern man's divorce of public practice from private profession.

Here one will not truly comprehend the present situation without a backward glance at certain major developments in American life as a whole during the past half century.

We are familiar with the Hegelian interpretation of history as a continuous process of action and reaction issuing in advance through the three successive phases of thesis, antithesis and synthesis. And we have already seen reason to recognize a measure of truth in this view. For purposes of analysis it is a useful framework in which to set the major currents of American history in recent times. Those currents may be interpreted in terms of three fairly clearly demarked periods which we may speak of as the Background, the Foreground, and the Present Situation.

I

The Background of our contemporary religious world is the America of the late nineteenth century—the America of the closing decades of the Victorian Era. No one can possibly understand the United States of today who has not achieved some imaginative grasp of the life and thought of that period. That is no easy

task even for those of us who are its grandchildren.[8]
With the exception of a very limited area on the At-
lantic seaboard, it was still a pioneer America. Its
energies were intensely preoccupied with the conquest
of the land, the taming of Nature's wilderness and
man's crude passions, the laying of the most elementary
foundations of great urban metropolises, of an industrial empire, of fabulous financial fortunes, of education and culture and civilized society. Its taste of the
lush fruits of its efforts was largely anticipatory. For
the most part, life was still strenuous, precarious, primitive. To its children this generation bequeathed the
enjoyment of its conquests, and it gloried in anticipat-
ing the opportunities which it was making possible for
them.

From the point of view of our interest, three characteristics of that generation are especially important.

a. One is the almost unimaginable poverty of its intellectual and cultural life. The great majority of those
who rose to foremost leadership in business, in community and state affairs, even in national affairs, were
without university education; many without full
schooling. Not infrequently their homes boasted not
over a dozen books, including a cheap and popular
compendium of knowledge with pages uncut, and
none of the world's great classics. Their comprehen-

---

[8] Much the most helpful introduction to the America of this period is
through Mark Sullivan's five-volume history, *Our Times,* especially Vols.
I and II—an invaluable portrait of an almost forgotten America.

sion of contemporary events was fashioned by their local newspaper with perhaps one item of international news each week. The horizons of their thought and conversation were strictly bounded by immediate and practical and local interests. In their homes, the literal word of Scripture was revered as verbally inspired— hardly less, the moral mores of the last generation, the world outlook of the local paper, and the traditional politics of the Republican (or Democratic) Party.

b. A second unmistakable characteristic of that generation was the absolute and unchallenged centrality of religion for them. By no means is this to suggest that religion actually succeeded in permeating every aspect of their life, as we shall have occasion to note in a moment. Rather, its position in their estimation and their intention was absolutely central. The influence of religion upon education furnishes an excellent indication of their conviction in this matter. As is well known, higher education in the United States was originally almost exclusively under Christian auspices. Colleges were mainly of two types—the older institutions which have since developed into the great privately endowed universities, most of them founded primarily as training schools for the ministry, their presidents, until recently, usually ordained clergymen; and the so-called "Christian colleges"—much smaller institutions scattered in every corner of the land, founded by individual religious communions and still in most instances under church supervision. Only in the second period did secular higher education attain significant proportions. Generally speaking, the relation of religion to education in the early period was twofold— religion was the sponsor and parent of education; and religion was the keystone of the educational arch, the determining consideration in educational theory and policy. This was precisely as most Americans wished. The place of religion in the education of their children exactly mirrored the place they professed to give it in their own lives.

c. With the third characteristic we approach very close to the heart of our contemporary problem. The practice of that generation was marked by a sharp divorce between the ethics of personal life and the ethics of public life.

In their private lives, our grandfathers' attitudes were a curious blend of romantic sentimentalism and puritan moralism. Each was rooted in their religion. There is a tendency today to forget how powerful was the romantic tinge in the outlook of that generation. They were sentimental in their thought of Nature. Gene Stratton Porter recalls the following incident on her first day at school.[9] The teacher had told her to read:

> "Birds in their little nests agree,
> And why can't we?"

[9] In her autobiographical novel, *Laddie.* (Copyright, 1913, by Doubleday, Doran & Company, Inc., New York. Published in London by John Murray.)

This is her description of the sequel:

" 'B-i-r-d-s, birds, i-n, in, t-h-e-i-r, their, l-i-t-t-l-e, little, n-e-s-t-s, nests, a-g-r-e-e, agree' . . . I followed the point of her pencil, while, a letter at a time, I spelled aloud my first sentence. . . .

"As I repeated the line, Miss Amelia . . . sprang to her feet, tripped a few steps toward the centre of the platform, and cried: 'Classes, attention! Our Youngest Pupil has just completed her first sentence. This sentence contains a Thought. It is a wonderfully beautiful Thought. A Thought that suggests a great moral lesson for each of us. "Birrds—in their little nests—agreeee." There is a lesson in this for all of us. We are here in our schoolroom like little birds in their nests. Now how charming it would be if all of us would follow the example of the birds, and at our work, and in our play, agreeee—be kind, loving, and considerate of each other. Let us all remember always this wonderful truth: "Birrrds—in their little nests—agreeeee." '

"In three steps I laid hold of her apron. . . . 'Ho but they don't!' I cried. 'They fight like anything! Every day they make the feathers fly!'

"In a backward stroke Miss Amelia's fingers, big and bony, struck my cheek a blow that nearly upset me. A red wave crossed her face, and her eyes snapped. I never had been so surprised in all my life. I was only going to tell her the truth. What she had said was altogether false. Ever since I could remember I had watched courting male birds fight all over the farm. . . . If a young bird failed to get the bite it wanted, it sometimes grabbed one of its nestmates by the bill, or the eye even. Always the oldest and strongest climbed on top of the youngest and fooled his mammy into feeding him most by having his head highest, his mouth widest, and begging loudest. There could be no mistake. I was so amazed I forgot the blow, as I stared at the fool woman.

"'I don't see why you slap me!' I cried. 'It's the truth! Lots of times old birds pull out bunches of feathers fighting, and young ones in the nests bite each other until they squeal.'

"Miss Amelia caught my shoulders and shook me.

"'Take your seat!' she cried. 'You are a rude, untrained child!'

"'They do fight!' I insisted, as I held my head high and walked to my desk."

They were sentimental in their romanticizing of national history. The American nation had never done wrong. Each of her wars was a war of defense and of righteousness—even the Mexican War! They were romantic in their view of national heroes. Washington was that paragon of holiness who had never told a lie. Lincoln was conceived in Messianic proportions. They were naïvely romantic in their assumption of the divine destiny of their country, their certainty of its inevitable prosperity and unending progress. A visitor from abroad thus characterized them:

"The Americans are filled with such an implicit and absolute confidence in their Union and in their future success that any remark other than laudatory is inacceptable to the majority of them. We have had many opportunities of hearing public speakers in America cast doubts upon the very existence of God and of Providence, question the historic nature or veracity of the whole fabric of Christianity; but never has it been our fortune to catch the slightest whisper of doubt, the slightest want of faith, in the chief God of America—unlimited belief in the future of America." [10]

They were, of course, profoundly sentimental in their conception of love and marriage. They were equally romantic in their religion—with simple and naïve faith, neat and complete certainties.

However, compounded with romantic sentimentality, was a rigid Christian puritanism in personal morals. This it is which, with all its shortcomings, has given to the present generation of American youth probably the sturdiest, healthiest, most disciplined physical inheritance to be found in all the world. The achievements of the succeeding period owed their possibility to the rugged manhood and womanhood wrought of an exacting and uncompromising self-discipline.

It was indeed a curious blend—romantic sentimentalism and puritan moralism. In each feature were the seeds of the subsequent revolt of the younger generation. As Mark Sullivan observes, "Requiring children to pretend to believe what they knew wasn't so, was food for the iconoclastic rebellion of youth that came into full flower many years later." [11] And the focal point of youth's attack was upon the rigid puritanism of their forebears. The important point, however, is that, whether the romantic or the puritan strain pre-

[10] Emil Reich, *Success Among the Nations,* quoted in Herbert Croly, *The Promise of American Life,* p. 1.
[11] *America Finding Herself,* p. 28.

dominated, the personal morality of our forefathers was dominated by their religious ideal and their Christian consecration.

Now turn to their public ethic—the habitual, usually unchallenged, actual practice of those same pious and revered persons in their business and political affairs. What a contrast!

They prided themselves upon the religious foundations of the national life. "Of course, ours is a Christian nation! Do we not recognize God in our Constitution? Do we not invoke God's blessing upon every great national decision, every important national anniversary? Do we not plead his guidance at the opening of each day's session of Congress?" Did the nation ever have a more consistent and impressive exponent of its national piety, clothing every public action with moving pleas for divine approval, confessing a continual personal dependence upon the divine support, than that majestic figure of a later period, Warren Gamaliel Harding—to whom perhaps more than to any other single individual we owe the chaos of the Prohibition era, the despoiling of the national treasury, profligacy in public expenditure, the betrayal and discrediting of public office, the extremity of the Depression, and the host of other social ills which dog our heels today? But we should not be too severe upon the memory of Mr. Harding. He was a very fair symbol of the generation which placed him in office and which gloried in the nation's affluence under his benign leadership.

Of course our grandfathers were profoundly religious men! Were they not stalwart and faithful pillars of the churches—attending public worship with scrupulous regularity, contributing generously from their plenty to the churches' enterprises at home and abroad, rearing their children in the fear of God and loyalty to his church, with family prayers, family pew and family piety? Yes, but how did they achieve their prosperity, these pious forebears of ours? How did they amass the fortunes which made their generous benefactions possible? How did they erect the vast business structure which was the main object of their consecrated devotion, the great joy of their pride, and the principal subject of their heartfelt gratitude to a beneficent Providence—that business structure which is crumbling around their descendants' ears today? What was the actual relation between the pious professions of their personal lives and the habitual working assumptions of their public activity?

Let us see the answer in the builders of our great family fortunes. What shall we say of one of the nation's foremost bankers who, on his biennial pilgrimage to the national convention of his church, filled his private car with bishops, and who is reported to have said that when he left his pew in a fashionable New York church each Sunday morning he folded his religion up like a napkin and placed it carefully beneath his pew to be removed at eleven o'clock the following Sunday morning; he could find no place for it in the hurly-burly of Wall Street where were his weekday preoccupations? Or, of several of the nation's greatest monarchs of business to whom almost every important educational and religious institution in the country is indebted for lavish largess—men whose fortunes were accumulated by as ruthless methods as modern business has known, by the simple expedient of destroying—through forthright cutthroat murder if possible, but if not through secret bribery, blackmail and the hiring of professional business gangsters— every struggling competitor? Or of one of the best known and best loved political and commercial leaders of the period who journeyed home from Washington faithfully each Saturday night to lead the largest men's bible class in a great eastern city each Sunday morning, but whose administration of a government department was said to be one of the most corrupt in a long succession of rather sordid records? [12]

To be sure, not all Christian business men and political leaders of that generation are to be thought of in terms of these giants of commerce and government. Such a generalization would be palpably unfair to

---

[12] Any one who harbors the suspicion that this picture may be overdrawn should consult Matthew Josephson, *The Robber Barons,* where the evidence is clearly set forth. The above was written before the appearance of Mr. Josephson's book. The examples selected are by no means the most striking ones.

thousands upon thousands of honest, upright laymen who toiled honorably to establish a modest fortune and gave without stint of mind and heart as well as purse to the furtherance of every good enterprise. Would any one question, however, that the illustrations given were fairly representative of an increasingly prevailing philosophy and practice of Christian life? Their recognized status, in the business world, in politics, *and* in the Church, is sufficient answer. They were the Herculean masters of industry and finance, proud symbols of the national success, examples for the emulation of every ambitious youngster. Yes, more than that. They were the foremost lay leaders of the Church—revered spokesmen on rare occasions when they could be prevailed upon to take its pulpit or platform, omniscient counsellors in all great issues of its welfare, indispensable financial guarantors of its mission of expansion at home and abroad.

Here is one of the keys to an understanding of present-day America, and certainly of its religious problem. It is the grandchild of an ancestry which was idealistic, chivalrous, puritanical, deeply pious in personal profession; often avaricious, unprincipled, Shylockian, utterly selfish in professional and political practice—romantic and moralistic in private life, ruthless and unscrupulous in public life. At the heart of the religion of that generation was a radical if unconscious insincerity. Such radical inconsistency was bound sooner or later to appear and destroy the pretensions of those in whom it dwelt. It did. As we should expect, the lower elements triumphed. This America made way for the America of the last two decades—the *Foreground* of the present picture. Romantic Moralism gave place to the Jazz Age.

2

The outlines of that *Foreground* are too familiar to require delineation. Many of its important features have occupied us in the preceding chapter.

The period was marked by the culmination and fruition of the earlier enterprises, a widespread enjoyment of the fruits of their labor. Expansion continued apace, achieved its maximum healthy limit, and overreached itself. Wealth mounted and multiplied, titillated men's avarice, and dissipated itself in luxurious and self-destructive extravagance. Ambition waxed, tasted success, and flowered in extravagant and absurd pretensions.

Directly parallel was the rapid secularization of American life. Here, again, developments in the field of education clearly revealed the whole situation. Education shared the movement of expansion. As recently as 1907 students in colleges and universities numbered about 300,000. By 1927 there were almost four times as many. Such increase in clientele could be handled only by a mushroom growth of institutions, of varied sizes and types, under a variety of auspices, in every section of the country. Gigantic state schools supported by public funds and often with no religious acknowledgment whatever now harbor perhaps a majority of the college youth. The old established privately endowed universities have sloughed off every vestige of ecclesiastical control or religious connection; their deference to religion, if any, is in no small measure a dutiful memorial to a respected past. The "Christian Colleges" are increasingly uncomfortable and embarrassed in their religious obligations; no longer is religion the keystone in their educational arch but one brick among many, and a brick for which a very logical or satisfactory or permanent place in the main structure has not been discovered. Thus has something like a revolution occurred within a single generation. It is an illuminating symbol of what was transpiring in the real religious outlook of the nation itself. Still, the place of religion in the education of their children accurately registers the position which most Americans wish it to have in their own lives.

With mercurial changes in the dimensions of American education have gone kaleidoscopic developments in educational theory. The new philosophy was born of the times. Its presuppositions, norms and objectives in considerable measure mirrored the secular mind. It shared American life's glorification of the individual, its disparagement of the past, its trust in science as mankind's Messiah, its unchallenged certainty of the fated prosperity and progress of the nation, its estimate of the true values of life, its non-religious premises, its incurable optimism, above all its confidence in man's power to know and to do—its this-worldly perspective. As fully as in the preceding period, education reflected the dominant convictions and desires of the national mind.

Most important, the dichotomy between profession and practice which had been apparent in the earlier generation widened. Moral discipline increasingly slackened. Religious profession became more and more perfunctory, irrelevant, insincere. The motives and goals and temper of the Modern Age won an ever stronger domination over the soul of the average citizen. Outwardly, the life of the typical American was marked by plenty, success, exuberant and expansive self-confidence; inwardly, by deepening unreality, uncertainty and threatened disintegration.

3

The Jazz Age issued, inevitably, in the *Present Situation,* which we have already reviewed in some detail.

4

The bearing of all this upon the vitality of men's faith in God may not at first appear. Let us come frankly to grips with the facts of contemporary thought about God. What do we present-day Christians really believe about God, and especially God's relation to society? Oh, not our professed beliefs. Not the declarations of our creeds. Or our pious assertions when we are gravely questioned and have ample time to think out our reply. What are our underlying assumptions— the assumptions which actually influence us as we move about our daily affairs? Here is the test question —Where do you and I think that we discover God? Where do we feel ourselves meeting him face to face?

Each one of us lives out his life in three concentric circles or spheres at the very centre of which he himself stands, each circle of wider radius than its predecessors. To be sure, of this fact we may be quite unaware. Nevertheless, at every moment each of us *is* surrounded by these three circles, each very different, and is in intimate relation with them. Indeed, it is the impact of these spheres upon us which *makes* our life.

The first—the realm of private experience—embraces the most intimate concerns of each man's inner life and his personal relationships. Here focus many of the deepest and most vital happenings of life—friendships, love and marriage and children and home, all those interior hopes and worries, dreams and disappointments, temptations and satisfactions which each of us holds within his own spirit, known only to himself and perhaps a few chosen confidants. Here what happens in the busy world of public affairs beyond touches him but secondarily.

The third circle concerns man's relationship to Nature, and to that vast, mysterious, silent, impenetrable Reality which furnishes the final but rather dim background of all that we are and all that we do—the encompassing environment of each man's life, and of mankind's drama. To this Reality we may feign indifference. It is, none the less, the very element in which we live and move and have our being, without whose changeless dependability and shrewd ordering, our petty existence could not continue through two successive instants.

There is an intermediate circle, however. It is the sphere of man's corporate relationships with his fellows —in work, in business, in industry, in government, in community and national life—all that we include when we speak of 'society.' It is the realm of history. We need no proof that it is in this intermediate circle that the great interests and energies of the nineteenth and twentieth centuries have been mainly concentrated. It is here that the most characteristic leaders of the period have lived out their lives.

Now, where is it that you and I find God? Where do we detect his operation, his touch upon human life? What is the message of God which the churches in the Modern Age have been giving to men? Where have they been told that they may expect to discover him? Primarily, in two places, is it not? In Nature, and in the intimacies of their own souls. But not in society.

Not a few of our contemporaries who disclaim all connection with formal religion still recognize the certainty of *some* Cosmic Power behind the great and mysterious Universe which envelopes and sustains them. Again, some among our contemporaries would affirm that they had met God face to face within their own spirits. In brief, we have come increasingly to think of God as the Author of Nature and possibly the solicitous Comforter of the solitary spirit; but not as the Sovereign of society, the moral Arbiter of men's corporate affairs. A God of cosmic order and power, and a God of love; but not a God of social righteousness, the God of history. We actually believe in a God who functions in but two of the three spheres in which each man dwells—the outermost and the innermost. The control and destiny of the intermediate circle—men's life in society, the realm where the concerns of our day so largely centre—has been left strictly to men's own devices. Is not that, in fact, our practical, working belief in the matter?

This was not the conviction of the fathers of old. We know that. For them God was the God of history. His living command ruled not merely the welfare of individuals but the destiny of nations and of generations. His righteous will for mankind prevailed in spite of and, if necessary, over the wilful purposes of men and parties. The divine hand determined the ultimate issue of all temporal events, corporate as well as individual. And that determination was for the vindication of truth and right. He was not merely a God of love whom one might know in personal friendship. He was equally the God of truth and right whom one must acknowledge in the flux of human events. For the God of history was pre-eminently a God of righteousness. His meaning for mankind was summed up in the conception of an overarching divine Providence.

Today men do not believe in such a God. In his social destiny man must work out his own salvation. To be sure, modern religion has had its 'Social Gospel'; but it has told us what we as Christians ought to do, not what God may or will do.

This is not the place to test the validity of the traditional belief or to expose the shortcomings of the modern substitute; that will concern us later.[13] Suffice it to say that, in their great basic certainty, the fathers of old were essentially right. The stupidity and absurdity of our error is revealed in any of three ways—by the sheer logic of the matter, by the brute facts of human history, by the tragic experience of recent events.

Here is a second fundamental failing in contemporary faith—not in men's theory but in their practice;

[13] See below, pp. 108–133.

in the unchallenged ethical procedures of their corporate life; in their tacit denial of the reign of God in human society.

V

The two sources of inadequacy in men's thought of God already mentioned—the approach to God by the outlook and method of science only, and the denial of God's regnancy in social affairs—are caught up in what we earlier fastened upon as the root failing in the whole outlook of the Modern Age—its distorted estimate of man. Modern religion has shared Modern Thought's homocentric perspective. It has been sure of the glory of a man, a little uncertain of the existence of God. It has loved to picture man—most learned, most earnest, most competent—pressing his arduous and baffled quest toward the dubious divine Reality. And God, in that picture? The whole perspective is absurd.

What *is* the situation of modern man? We see him clearly as he has imagined himself—an autonomous, self-sufficient, masterful figure, set down at the very centre of a world of which he has made himself undisputed sovereign. And we see him clearly as he actually is—an isolated, impoverished, dwarfish, futile creature, without vital relationship to all that could give his existence depth and meaning and strength and beauty. Here is the last abstraction—man himself.

Man divorced from his own past, as we have discovered Modern Thought severing him, is an abstraction.

Man employing the abstract symbols of modern business or schooled in the abstract concepts of modern science is an abstraction.

Man divorced from intimate relationships of mutual responsibility and dependence with his fellow-men, as modern urban civilization has placed him, is an abstraction.

Man at his work divorced from an organic process and from the sense of creative accomplishment in his labor, as modern industry has tethered him, is an abstraction.

Man divorced from the imperious compulsion of moral necessity, as modern society has cushioned him, is an abstraction.

Man divorced from vivid awareness of the cosmic setting of his existence, as the modern temper has dulled him, is an abstraction.

Man divorced from the dim murmur of infinite spaces, from the brooding enfoldment of an eternity beyond time, from the haunting sense of a personal destiny beyond the stumbling trivialities of this mortal come and go, is an abstraction.

Man divorced from the initial Source of his being and the immediate Sustainer of his hopes and the final Arbiter of his fortune is an abstraction.

And the result of such pervasive and controlling abstraction upon the life of man? It has been well described by one of the most acute interpreters of our contemporary problem:

"The organic structure of life is hierarchical, that is, cosmic, and in the cosmic organism the parts submit to the whole and all depend on the centre. The centre is the last end, the object, of the life of the parts. If the parts of an organism break away from the whole and cease to look to their centre they insensibly come under the control of a lower kind of nature. . . . Human powers that escape from a state of organism inevitably become enslaved to mechanization.

"Human identity, like every authentic reality, is only conferred in that spiritual concretion which puts the seal of divine unity on the whole of human multiplicity. In abstraction and isolation it is lost. The process of modern Humanism is the passage from man in this spiritualized concretion, where everything is organically bound together, to a sundering abstraction, wherein man is changed into an isolated unit. Man expected to find freedom, to confirm his individuality, and to acquire creative energy by thus passing from the concrete to the abstract. He wanted to free himself—by shaking off that divine grace which had gone to the making of his own image and which spiritually fed him. Abstract humanism is a breaking-away from and a denial of grace, whereas life is concrete only in grace, outside it is abstract.

"The man of later history is forced to wander about on the surface of life, and on that surface, cut off from all communion with the depths, he will have to do what he can with his own effective powers. . . . The natural man alone cannot draw from inexhaustible springs for his creativeness: he drains himself dry, and only the arid surface of life is left. . . . When man broke away from the spiritual moorings of his life he tore himself from the deeps and went to the surface, and he has become more and more superficial. When he lost the spiritual centre of Being he lost his own at the same time." [14]

In discovering the secret of our plight, we find also the final and basic reason for our decline of faith. Man without God is an abstraction. And man, become an abstraction, inevitably loses God.

VI

However, it will not do merely to reveal inadequacies in prevalent ways of thinking. Analysis is not enough. The obligation is upon us to propose alternative and truer perspectives. What, in briefest outline, would be indispensable premises in the Christian message of the Living God? Let us speak of four.

1. The Primacy of Religion in Life

We have traced the mutations in religion's fortune within the modern period. We have noted its grad-

---

[14] Nicholas Berdyaev, *The End of Our Time* (Sheed and Ward, Inc.), pp. 42, 41, 37, 22, 25, 17. I have taken the liberty of rearranging the passages. *Cp.* C. G. Jung, *Modern Man in Search of a Soul*, p. 247. "Whether from the intellectual, the moral, or the æsthetic viewpoint, the undercurrents of the psychic life of the West present an uninviting picture. We have built a monumental world round about us, and have slaved for it with unequalled energy. But it is so imposing only because we have spent upon the outside all that is imposing in our natures—and what we find when we look within must necessarily be as it is, shabby and insufficient."

ually altered status, both in the common life and in the personal loyalty of its adherents. For there are two distinct aspects of religion's position always—the place conceded it in the general outlook, and the influence which it actually wields among those who are its avowed supporters. A significant fact about recent developments is that one can detect no marked difference in religion's importance in these two settings. Its functioning influence in the lives of its followers has changed very largely as its place in the estimate of the general attitude has altered. In both alike, and with fairly direct parallel, it has passed from a position of recognized centrality to one of important but distinctly secondary influence, and then to the status of a quite incidental and peripheral concern.

The present prevailing position of religion—its actual influence in society, to be sure; but, much more important, the place it holds in the devotion of those who profess its loyalty—is altogether unreal. Religion may be untrue. In that case, it is dangerous. It is never incidental. To assign it to any such status is to falsify the whole situation. Religion is central or it is nothing at all. We have already urged that, if there be a God, he cannot be one among other more or less interesting factors in the Universe. Rather he must be the one primal and supremely significant fact—in relation to which all others must be oriented and given their significance. Only when we so think of him are we thinking of GOD. By the same token, if religion be man's relation to that unique and primal Reality, it *must* be a matter of central and utterly unique concern. If we think of it as a quite casual affair, or if we in fact grant it an incidental importance in life, it is not RELIGION with which we have to do, but some cheap and inconsequential counterfeit. For it is not relationship to GOD which is occupying our attention.

It may be objected, "This is all well enough in theory. But, come, be practical. Recognize that there is no reasonable possibility of securing for religion its rightful recognition in the popular mind. In days like these, religion had best be content with whatever notice it can obtain, and be thankful." To which, the reply should be, "Forget the popular mind. The numbers of those who give formal acknowledgment to religion is, at most, a comparatively secondary consideration. What really matters is the power it holds in the loyalty and conviction of those who profess its allegiance."

In the end of the day, it may be seen that the churches have been mistaken in encouraging men to continue in nominal affiliation, when they had contentedly relegated religion to a quite minor attention. Possibly it is better that men frankly be warned that they can have no recognition from the institution whose responsibility it is to represent the Ultimate Reality within the common life, unless they give to that Reality the only appropriate recognition. It is better to tell men that it is not RELIGION to which they are rendering perfunctory acknowledgment than· to encourage them in insincere and futile false-profession. Certainly the churches have been mistaken, and basely disloyal to their mission, in permitting people to think this an adequate service to religion, and in rejoicing in the fragments of important men's attention which they were successful in claiming. The apostasy of the churches is not that they allowed religion to come into its present trivial position in the corporate estimate— that was a development largely beyond their control; but that they acquiesced in the common attitude and accommodated themselves to its acceptance. Above all, it has been blameworthy in the churches tacitly to link their own appraisal of religion's significance with the position it happens to hold in popular esteem, thereby furthering the parallel between religion's status in general opinion and its status in the loyalties of avowed adherents. For it is the clear testimony of history that *living* religion is *always* the possession of a numerically inconsequential minority within a community which, whatever its lip service to formal religion, is, at the springs of its life, through and through secular. The power of RELIGION within society is not in the nominal and largely unthinking recognition of the masses (the fact that their recognition *is* formal and unthinking means that it is not RELIGION with which they have to do), but in the true devotion of those, many or few, who know in their spirits what RELIGION is and, by the quality of their devotion, represent its reality truly before the eyes of all.

2. *The Priority of God in Experience*

We have argued that any one who thinks of God as an 'object,' one object among other objects, an 'It' among other 'its,' cannot possibly make sure of him. It is not GOD to which attention is directed. God, if there be a God, *must* be the one primal and supremely significant fact. Only if he be sought in his true nature, can he ever be discovered and verified by the human spirit. Moreover, we adduced considerations of very obvious common-sense in support of this position.

There is a further implication to which the same common-sense guidance clearly points. We have reminded ourselves of the familiar and favorite posture of the modern mind, pressing its intent and laborious quest through encompassing mystery in the general direction of a dubious divine reality. We have noted that such an attitude assumes, whether deliberately or unconsciously, that God is a distant and wholly passive object toward which man's mind must feel its baffled way as best it can. We have hinted that this whole point of view is palpably grotesque, indeed just a little ridiculous—a lampoon possible only for a mind in which egoism had almost swallowed up all sense of humor, and so all wisdom. God, if there be a God, must be the most living, pregnant, potent of beings—'an ever-present, ever-active, all-encompassing Reality which gives to our seeking minds such reality as they possess, making insistent and never-wearied impact upon them.' He must be the prior Provoker of all our seeking. Only if it be acknowledged that so he must be, is it likely that he will ever be truly apprehended and made sure of.

What *is* the situation of man with regard to that Something which he aims to understand and with which he longs to enter into fellowship? It is that of a creature, standing like a child, before a majestic mysterious REALITY whose dimensions he can never begin accurately to comprehend and whose precise nature and purpose he may never hope fully to know. We moderns are in the habit of defining what God *should* be, that is, what we insist that he shall be if we are to grant him worship; and then we probe about if haply we may feel after such a One and find him. Rather, we must *acknowledge* God—that mysterious, ineffable, never-fully-knowable, never-to-be-completely-understood, always-more-fully-to-be-apprehended Being who sometimes seems to hover—austere, inscrutable, severe—behind the majesty and grandeur of Nature. Then like Job of old, we must struggle in our soul's suffering and perplexity to be certain that we can confide all our hopes and visions to him whom by necessity we must recognize and obey. The great question for man is not, "Is there a God, that is, an Ultimate Reality far exceeding our powers of comprehension and in whose hands our destiny resides?" but "Is the God, whose existence we are compelled to acknowledge, good?"

"That there is an Administration of the Universe cannot be denied. Something has determined and continues to determine the functioning of natural law, the orderly transformations of matter and energy. . . . From one point of view the question 'Is there a God?' is promptly and finally answered in the affirmative. But that is not the real question at issue. Man wants to know the character of this Administration of the Universe which he is obliged to accept whether it pleases him or not. He yearns to discover the true nature of the determining Something. The real question is, 'What sort of God is it which rules this world?' " [15]

The predicament of Job is a far sounder starting-point for the soul's great pilgrimage than the self-conscious arrogance of the man of today.

The beginning of religion—the only beginning which gives to any of us promise of a successful outcome— is the attitude of one who bows, awestruck, helpless, penitent, wondering, before the Divine Majesty. That is the sound beginning, not because it is a beautiful or pious or trusting attitude, but for the sole and sufficient

[15] Kirtley Mather, in *The Forum Magazine*, January, 1929.

reason that it precisely corresponds with the truth of the matter. For we do stand, all of us, whenever wisdom guides our minds to sane humility, face to face with the great Divine Majesty who is the Sovereign of our fate and before whom we must sit down as little children—to learn, and to worship. If that Majesty come to us, as it did to the Prodigal, in the forgiveness of a Parent's unwearied affection and faith, so much the better. If it come to a wayward generation like our own in the judgment of a stern Disciplinarian, it has come in that fashion of old to better men than we. This, I suspect, is the deeper meaning of the present suffering of our civilization. God is seeking to teach us through the hard, hard measures he has heaped upon the sons of men through the ages that he *must* be acknowledged as GOD if he is to be known and loved as the Giver of our peace.

To say the same thing in somewhat more formal fashion—the starting-point in men's apprehension of God is the recognition of a transcendent, mysterious and immensely potent Other. Only later are they likely to become quite certain that that Other is personal Love; perhaps still later, that he is perfect Goodness. Here, the analogy from childhood may be suggestive. Is it not true that, to childhood's impression, a parent is recognized first as mere 'person,' then as 'love'; and that both of these apprehensions come long before his ethical character can be fully appreciated?

74

To be sure, we have been speaking here only of men's initial awareness of God. This is *only* the starting-point. At the far end, beckons that intimate comradeship with One who is the very Life of our souls and the Confidant of our hearts' secret longings which, through the radiant reality of the saints, we know to be possible for the best of men, and which each of us has foretasted flittingly within his own experience. It is the true and sound perspective, prerequisite to the soul's mature discoveries, which we have here been concerned to stress. For that perspective is of prime importance.

When men sincerely take up this attitude, the perspective of wisdom and common-sense, truth is made known to them—never easily or completely, but as much and as rapidly as their spirits are competent to receive. What is required of them if they are to make entrance into the Kingdom of light and life is not primarily profound answers to their baffled questioning, but an utterly new stance on the questioners' part —a stance from which revealing light may become clearly apparent.

So the great spirits of the centuries have found themselves in the certainty of the Divine Presence. Often, their perplexities have remained. To many of their questions they have gotten no complete and omniscient answers. Indeed, in their new faith they have desired none. The final authority for this faith has been their

lives' insistent certainty where God has spoken to them
face-to-face. And that certainty has come as they have
bowed, in penitence and in wonder and in high expectation, before him. With Job they have cried out,
"Though he slay me, yet will I trust him." And then,
"I know that my Redeemer liveth." And, at the end,
"I had heard of thee by the hearing of the ear. But
now mine eye seeth thee."

3. *The Manifold Impact of God upon Our Life*

Many people's hold upon God is after the manner
of a chain of interlocking links. To be sure, only with
the most earnest and reflective is the chain finely
wrought and carefully welded. With most, it is a
rough and ready makeshift. The links are of very
varying size and strength. But somehow, they hold
together. It is their combined reach which connects
men with the Divine. True to the proverb, the chain
is as strong as its weakest link. Let one link fail, and
the chain falls slack and useless. Living connection
with God is severed.

Indeed, the whole persuasion of Modern Thought
has been to urge us so to think of religious certainty.
Men's certainty of God, it has said, depends on a neatly
and carefully developed chain of reasoning, in which
each consideration follows logically from its predeces-
sor and hangs upon it. The ideal result is a beautifully

welded structure of argument. And—men's certainty is as secure as the weakest argument. Let one link in the chain break or be threatened, and the validity of the whole is destroyed. Men are left—faith-less.

As a matter of fact, any such conception of the nature of our hold upon God is utterly mistaken. The ties which join man's life to the Divine are not one but many. If we are seeking a figure, they are not of the nature of a welded chain in which the strength of the whole rests upon the strength of each link. Rather, they may be likened to a cordon, woven of many quite separate and different strands, each with its individual and independent strength. Very varied these strands are—some formed from the crude but tough fibres of Nature, others from the delicate and fragile threads of inmost experience. As we should expect, it is the most delicate strands in the rope of faith which are most highly prized. Often, however, it is the coarse and rough fibres which are sturdiest and most secure, best proof against the stresses and strains of human weather and the testing blows of fate.

To be sure, study and reflection weave the diverse strands into an ordered unity. That is the work of the mind's incurable passion for coherence. Nevertheless, the pattern is never complete, the mind's effort at unification is never fully successful. That is a blessing. It is vivid reminder that the ties between God and ourselves are, in their first appearance, independent and unconnected; and, to the end, they remain in some measure so. Upon one or another or another, our faith can trust for its security at different times, as occasion may demand. For our linkage to God is as secure as the *strongest* thread, as secure as the strongest thread at any particular moment in our life.

To say the same thing without metaphor, men's certainty of God rests, not upon a carefully constructed chain of logical reasoning, but upon a collection of relatively independent considerations, of very varying significance for us and of very varying rational strength. No one of them alone appears secure enough to give steady assurance, or strong enough to stand immovable against the more severe testings of adversity and doubt. It is the weight of them all, so many and so diverse evidences, in their common agreement which gives them overpowering persuasiveness. It is their united strength—not the unity of complete and mutually dependent cohesion but the unity of individually independent supports—which gives to religion's belief its impregnable certainty.[16] The imperturbable splendor and grandeur of the Universe; the imperious command of the highest; Beauty—the beauty of Nature without and that far more mysterious whisper of beauty within; the glory of a few human lives; the

---

16 See the very similar suggestion in A. E. Taylor, "The Vindication of Religion" in *Essays, Catholic and Critical*, pp. 63, 80. *Cp.*, also, William Temple, *Nature, Man and God*, p. viii.

face of Jesus Christ; the tale of human history; supremely, the enveloping Presence which speaks personally to each man one by one—these and others are the extraordinarily varied strands woven into the fabric of a rich and worthy certainty.

It is when a man's thought of God is formed of a single approach that it is impoverished and cheap, for the very good reason that his thought has hold of only a tiny fragment of the whole and therefore is sadly distorted. It is when a man's assurance of God hangs upon a single thread that his certainty is fragile and precarious. Men differ greatly in the appeal which the varied intimations of the Divine make to them. It is well that each one recognize and keep firm grip upon what is for him the strongest, the unbreakable, strand in the cordon of his faith. It is also well if he remind himself often of the other equally true and important strands which other men find alone sufficient, that these may be woven into the substance of his own conviction and so his faith may be both enriched and made secure.

Of these strands, so many and so varied, the toughest and most tenacious, because completely free from inner mood and tension, is that celebrated by the psalmist:

> "The heavens proclaim the glory of God,
> The firmament showeth his handiwork."

Some one has said that the ordinary man, his native insight uncontaminated by too much learning and false sophistication, will always be sure of a few things: the reality of some Power behind the cosmos, the difference between right and wrong, the claim of the right upon his devotion. In the first of these intuitive certainties, he is unquestionably on firm ground. Many a man of today who long since bade farewell to the life of the church suspects, in moments of random reflection, that behind the vast and impenetrable Nature which surrounds and supports his petty existence there must be some Great Cosmic Power. 'The starry heavens above' still speak to men of God. And, when they think they detect that voice in the heavens, they are not deceived. So long as man's mind retains one iota of perspective, he will continue to read the marks of the Most High in the Universe which bears and sustains and destroys him. Indeed, failure so to read the signs of the heavens is stark illustration of the distorted perspective of the Modern Mind.

Again, the untutored man is within reach of a second tried and strong cord of linkage with the Divine in his other intuitive assumptions—the difference between right and wrong and the absolute claim of the higher upon his devotion. There come times in the experience of most men when assurance of God grows desperately dim. Often, that uncertainty is only one element in a far more fundamental and drastic over-hauling of all life's convictions. It is a symptom of an infection which has spread its paralysis through every function of the mind's organism. Certainty of God is insecure; but certainty of almost everything else has become insecure at the same moment. Then the great question is not, "Am I sure of God?" but "Am I sure of anything?" If, in such a crisis, a man turn outward toward Nature, he may find steadiness and perspective in his confusion. More probably, the focus of his attention is glued within. Nature's majesty is too distant, too cold, too impersonal for his relief. Her imperturbable splendor serves rather to mock and harass his spirit's agitation. If he is to find secure standing-ground, it must be within that spirit's sickly confusion. Then he searches his soul for some single certainty on which he may lay firm hold as a foundation-stone for rebuilding. In such predicament, many a man has known the illumination which came to this Yale undergraduate, facing the annihilation of all conviction.

"Finally, pacing his chamber some day, there comes up the question, 'Is there, then, no truth that I do believe? Yes, there is this one, now that I think of it: there is a distinction of right and wrong that I never doubted, and I see not how I can; I am even quite sure of it.' Then forthwith starts up the question, 'Have I, then, ever taken the principle of right for my law? I have done right things as men speak; have I ever thrown my life out on the principle to become all it requires of me? No, I have not, consciously I have not. Ah! then, here is something for me to do! No matter what becomes of my questions— nothing ought to become of them if I cannot take a first principle so inevitably true, and live in it. Here, then, will I begin. If there is a God, as I rather hope there is, and very dimly believe, he is a right God. If I have lost him in wrong, perhaps I shall find him in right. Will he not help me, or, perchance, even be discovered to me?'"[17]

This may seem a meager foundation-stone for the rebuilding of conviction, a slim thread on which to hang the whole structure of faith. It is enough. In similar vein, one of the bravest spirits of the War generation, himself a minister who had brought cheer and faith to many in pain and in bereavement, wrote from France three weeks before his own death from battle-wounds:

"I am getting to care less and less whether a thing is so, whether it's reasonable, whether it's capable of proof. If it's fine, if it lifts you above the realms of self into the realm of sacrifice, why, darn it, it should be true! If it isn't, it's not your fault and you have the chance of getting even with the maker of a universe who was too stupid to include it, by pretending and acting as if it were true. And in pretending and acting, I suspect one is more apt than not to acquire an insight into its worthwhileness as a guide for living, which you can never get by sitting down on the outside and studying the thing objectively. In so doing it

[17] Horace Bushnell, *Life and Letters*, p. 58. The passage is autobiographical.

becomes the truth for you, if you are still sufficiently sophis-
ticated to care about its truth or untrueness." [18]

It is enough because it is sure; it does not change.
As Mazzini put it, "Whether the sun shine with the
serene splendor of an Italian noon, or the leaden
corpse-like hue of the northern mist be above us, I cannot see that it changes our duty." It is enough because
it is a promising beginning. It does not carry us into
the Presence of God—the moral imperative. It does set
our feet firmly in the right direction. More than that,
it places our paralyzed and powerless spirits within
the radius of an enormous energy of attraction which
may draw them from their morass and set them in
motion again. In response to that attraction, they may
recover themselves and press forward. Indeed, they
may finally discover that the energy which lifts them
from futility and pulls them along the way is the
strength of the Divine; the attraction to which their
beaten spirits make response is the moral Grandeur of
God. For the voice of conscience *is* the voice of God,
and the accents of gentleness and love may be detected only after we have done obedience to its imperious commands.

Once again, there are far more delicate and valued
threads which reassure us of our contact with God and

[18] Mrs. Parker Vanamee, *Vanamee* (Harcourt Brace and Co., Inc.),
p. 303.

his never-wearied touch upon us. Beauty—the beauty
in Nature which moved Wordsworth to the familiar
"Lines Composed a Few Miles Above Tintern Abbey."

> . . . "For I have learned
> To look on nature, not as in the hour
> Of thoughtless youth; but hearing oftentimes
> The still, sad music of humanity,
> Nor harsh, nor grating, though of ample power
> To chasten and subdue. And I have felt
> A presence that disturbs me with the joy
> Of elevated thoughts; a sense sublime
> Of something far more deeply interfused,
> Whose dwelling is the light of setting suns,
> And the round ocean and the living air,
> And the blue sky, and in the mind of man;
> A motion and a spirit, that impels
> All thinking things, all objects of all thought,
> And rolls through all things."

Likewise, that far more mysterious whisper of Beauty
within, which speaks to us in the silence whenever
our spirits are hushed to listen, persuading us of our
potential worth, tantalizing us with the promise of
things which never were on land or sea, and encouraging us to try to body forth these delicate intimations
for the eye and ear of men.

For Christians, however, evidence of equal delicacy
but far greater objectivity than command of duty or
whisper of beauty, and of complete objectivity but far
greater delicacy than the structure or beauty of Na-

ture is to be found always close at hand. It is—in the spirits of men and women. Not all men and women equally to be sure, but those especially in whom we recognize the destiny of human life to have achieved realization. This is Christianity's central and distinctive conviction—that in one of our humanity, one like unto ourselves, God drew near to men and made himself vividly certain to them. "The Word was made flesh and dwelt among us." Yes, but that is not all. It is the further conviction that God is forever and always afresh coming among men, taking flesh again, and dwelling with them in those like themselves. Because of the unmistakable presence of God in one human Life supremely, but because of his no less certain presence in other human lives, men shall be sure of him— that is the meaning of the Incarnation.

This is the only public proof of God which could be fully convincing or altogether satisfying—the reflection of his Presence in a fellow-man. Through human personalities alone could human beings find Divine Love made sure. In Blake's quaint phrase: "Think of a white cloud as being holy, and you cannot love it: think of a holy man within a white cloud and love springs in your thought: to think of holiness as distinct from man is impossible to the affections." There *are* some human lives, few though they be, who as we confront them make confidence in God inevitable. This climactic evidence is to be found not merely in the life of Jesus, but in many and many another. Perhaps most of all, in lives of utter simplicity and insignificance, as the world measures importance. To tighten grip on the reality of such lives is to reclaim certainty of God.

> "Through such souls alone
> God stooping shows sufficient of His light
> For us i' the dark to rise by." [19]

Finally, the most precious and delicate thread of all —and one of irrefragable security to those who have discovered it and will trust all to its strength—is the awakening to an enveloping Presence which speaks quietly and intimately to each spirit, one by one. Some faint suggestion of this Presence every man has sensed at times of rare reality. In the measure that reality dominates his life, the voice of that Presence becomes the nearly constant companion of his soul's solitude and the strong confirmer of its meaning and its hope.

Then, a man may make the ultimate confession of faith which is the true goal of the spiritual pilgrimage of each one of us:

> "O Lord, thou hast searched me and known me.
> Thou knowest my downsitting and mine uprising,
> Thou understandest my thought afar off. . . .
> Thou hast beset me behind and before,
> And laid thine hand upon me. . . .

[19] Robert Browning, *The Ring and the Book*, Pompilia's speech.

Whither shall I go from thy spirit?
Or whither shall I flee from thy presence?
If I ascend up into heaven, thou art there:
If I make my bed in hell, behold, thou art there.
If I take the wings of the morning,
And dwell in the uttermost parts of the sea;
Even there shall thy hand lead me,
And thy right hand shall hold me. . . .
Search me, O God, and know my heart:
Try me, and know my thoughts:
And see if there be any wicked way in me,
And lead me in the way everlasting." [20]

4. *The Regnancy of God in History*

In our sketch of these many and varied intimations, one which has had peculiar strength for Christian certainty whenever its insight has been clear and true has been omitted. It is the evidence of God's guiding and moulding influence upon the great drama of mankind's history. By no means is it the most important support of men's personal belief. It is, however, an *absolutely indispensable* element in their total apprehension of God. Without it, no thought of God can be sound and adequate. Its neglect for long, by any individual or generation, must lead to one of the strangling abstractions which are the precursors of spiritual sterility.

Clear conviction of the rule of God in history is the fourth condition for a recovery of the Christian message of God in our day. Moreover, of the essential

[20] Psalm 139.

premises suggested, this is the one which stands nearest to the centre of the concern of this book. It is upon this particular strand in the cord of faith that we shall focus attention in the following chapter.

CHAPTER THREE

THE MESSAGE IN SOCIETY'S CRISIS

CHAPTER THREE

THE MESSAGE IN SOCIETY'S CRISIS

At no time in the past half century has a message from the Christian Church for society's life been as desperately needed as it is today. At no time in the past half century has the voice of the Church in its social message been as uncertain, as incoherent, as unconvincing, as it is at this hour. This is the tragic paradox in the present situation of religion's influence upon public affairs.

I

Of the first aspect of the paradox—the urgent need that Christian forces should bring a clear, united and powerful message to the social issues of the time—few would be inclined to raise question. We look out upon a world in chaotic confusion and bewilderment. Its life is passing through an experience of profound gestation. At no time since the Armistice has another world-cataclysm threatened so imminently. We appear to hover on the brink of another World War. Not in many centuries has society's structure in its every aspect—its political institutions, its accepted economic theories and arrangements, its unquestioned intellectual axioms, its ideals and practices of public morality—

been so completely in the melting-pot as today. Each of the most cherished and unquestioned assumptions of the life of the modern world—the validity of democracy, the right of the individual to freedom of speech and judgment, the benefaction of modern civilization, the reality of progress, the practicability of Christian ideals in corporate life, the ability of men to build a decent world, to discover truth, to save their own souls—each is being called seriously in question. By many of our most competent guides, some of them are regarded as hopelessly obsolete. Not in many centuries has the future of the world's life, even the immediate future, been as completely unpredictable as it is today. It is possible that at this moment we are living in the death-pangs of a civilization, at one of the four or five greatest crises in all human history.

Many speak of this as a time of 'transition.' That is a quite inadequate description of the situation. 'Transition' suggests a stage in an orderly progress—for example, the passage from youth to manhood or womanhood which, with all of the familiar stresses and strains of adolescence, is a natural and desirable step in a regular development. The world's present agony is far more than that. If we are seeking analogies, it is more akin to premature widowhood or widowerhood—the harrowing devastation of one who has set life's course joyously and confidently in intimate comradeship with another, and then is bereft of the companion forever.

The whole structure of the experience and its hope are shattered. Never within the life of this generation will that happy promise be recovered or even approached. Never can the partner to our gladness and our day-dreams—prosperity, comfort, wealth—return to our embrace. Ultimately we may arrange some other and poorer alliance; but it will be felt as an adjustment of expediency and convenience. For us, life must *always* be accommodation to a cheap second-best. It is no 'transition' we are passing through. It is the tragic and painful reconciliation of a whole generation to a fate of deprivation, disillusion and despair. "We are entering into the realm of the unknown and the un-lived, and we are entering it joylessly and without much hope." [1]

We look out upon a world in chaotic confusion; that is serious. But that is not the whole of the picture. It is a world to which the most confident and powerful leadership is being supplied by non-christian philosophies and movements. As we said earlier, in every corner of the world causes and faiths are powerfully clamant for men's allegiance which speak with assurance, with finality, with dictation to our generation. They are giving precisely the definite and authoritative guidance which men expect from religion. Two such faiths command the complete devotion of millions of men across the face of the world today—nationalism

[1] Nicholas Berdyaev, *The End of Our Time*, p. 12.

and Communism. Antipodal as are their premises, their aims and their programs in many respects, they are strangely akin in many features more fundamental. Each possesses many clear marks of a religion—a gospel of sure salvation from chaos and despair for both individual and society; heroes worshipped as the saviors of their peoples; authoritative, almost verbally inspired, writings; dogma—clear, convinced, compelling; some measure of ritual; power to stir and direct tremendous latent emotional energies; the requirement of complete self-giving on the part of its adherents; intense and passionate partizanship; undiscouraged proselytism; vivid apocalyptic expectation. Each demands and wins a religious devotion from its members, and goes far toward satisfying the conscious spiritual needs of their souls. Each supplies to their minds a definite and confident proposal for society's transformation—its 'social gospel.' [2] To repeat—we look out upon a world in chaotic confusion; that is serious. We look out upon a confused world in which leadership is increasingly supplied by unchristian forces which function as religions for those who follow them; that is tragic.

This is one aspect of the paradox—the world's need

[2] Speaking of Communism, Berdyaev says, "Soviet philosophy is a theology: it has its revelation, its holy books, its ecclesiastical authority, its official teachers; it supposes the existence of one orthodoxy and innumerable heresies." *The End of Our Time*, p. 211. *Cp.* Basil Mathews, in *The Christian Message for the World Today* (A. L. Warnshuis, Editor). Chap. II.

for the Church's leadership. Meantime profound changes are taking place in the Church's social message—what is called the Social Gospel. No one can have failed to note the deepening uncertainty about it —what it is, what it means in terms of specific measures, how it is to be made effective in the life of society. The disillusionment which dogs today's life in every aspect has breathed its withering fog across the social vision of Christianity. The doubt which raises insistent question before every presupposition of the prevailing outlook is challenging the social ideals and programs of the churches. Were they not products, very typical products, of nineteenth-century romantic liberalism, it is asked? Is not that liberalism now wholly discredited? Should they not suffer the same fate which is rapidly felling each of the great secular assumptions and proposals of the period? Confidence in the adequacy and efficacy of the social message of Christianity is crumbling. It is conceded to have served its day— courageously, sincerely, usefully. Our debt to it is great. But it will no longer do.

One thing is clear. We are witnessing the disintegration of the traditional Social Gospel—the gospel which has claimed the intense devotion of the finest leaders and the nominal assent of the entire Christian Church for more than a quarter of a century. The most significant fact is that the movement of collapse is twofold. As with the whole outlook of the Modern Age, the disintegration is by a double catalysis—through external attack and through desertion within.

Among the recognized spokesmen of the social message of Christianity, there is rather more confusion, more uncertainty, more distrust of the traditional gospel than among its critics. They are no longer sure of their message—of the assumptions and proposals which heretofore have been fundamental and unchallenged axioms among them. They query whether religion may not be impotent to battle the evils of mankind's corporate life and to effect social salvation, even if it be not a positive narcotic as Communism maintains. They doubt the efficacy of love as a solvent of social injustice. They question the social importance of the Church. They feel themselves under heightened pressure from secular social philosophies which seek their allegiance—philosophies not so readily translated into Christian terms as was the idealistic liberalism which inspired their early enthusiasm. Above all, they discover themselves turning increasingly to secular political programs rather than to the professed ideals of Christianity for their message, and to secular social reformers rather than to fellow-Christians for leadership and comradeship in their social efforts.[3]

Meantime, throughout the Church, one seems to de-

---

[3] As is well known, the point of sorest dispute among interpreters of the Social Gospel concerns the Christian attitude toward the use of force. But that is only the most painful symptom of a general condition of strain and division.

tect a mounting distrust of *their* leadership. Men whose interpretation of social Christianity won ready acclaim five years ago confront scepticism, criticism, hostility. Their general influence among fellow-churchmen appears to be waning. The old query is being pressed anew—whether Christian leaders can be trusted to meddle in essentially political and economic matters.

In brief, at the very moment of the world's desperate need, the social influence of Christianity stands in critical crisis. By social reformers the validity and value of religion for social change is being severely challenged afresh. By practising Christians the wisdom and competence of social enthusiasts is being severely questioned today. And the Church speaks with a contradictory voice, feebly or not at all.[4]

This is the setting in which we approach our topic. It is no part of our purpose to attempt to restate Chris-

---

[4] Many friends of the Social Gospel will think this a one-sided and unfair picture of the present situation. They will cite not a few signs of growing agreement within the Church on social matters. For example, one critic reminds me that "the social relevance of Christianity is increasingly taken for granted by the church as a whole," that "there is a steady growth in the realization by large groups within the Church of the radical nature of the Christian criticism of society," and that spokesmen of the Social Gospel who speak with moderation and winsomeness are greeted with an increasingly cordial hearing.

I am very sympathetic with this correction and gratefully alive to the advances of the Church's social influence in some areas. For a complete picture, the above analysis would require much supplementation. I have sought to fasten upon the *most significant* current developments. If this book is right in its understanding of the general situation, they are likely to become increasingly characteristic of the whole life of the Church.

tianity's social message. Our aim is a far more modest one. It is threefold. First, to suggest why the Church's social message *must* be rethought and to stress its urgent importance; this we have just attempted to do. Second, to seek to define the presuppositions for a restatement of the Christian message for society in these times. Third, to point out certain distinctive and invaluable contributions which personal religion may be expected to furnish to the social task in any day. To the second question, we now turn.

II

Where is the fundamental source-spring of the Christian message to society? It is in the Christian conviction concerning history and God's relationship to history. Here are to be discovered the presuppositions of the Church's social message in any age. In the first instance, that message, like every other aspect of Christian insight, is a certainty concerning God.

In passing, it may be well to assure ourselves that there *is* a Christian philosophy of history, and to underscore the importance of its recovery in our time. Not a few churchmen, with the great bulk of secular reformers, might be inclined to echo a recent statement of a young Christian radical, "Of course, there is no such thing as a Christian philosophy of history." The declaration is absurd. To be sure, no two Christians are likely to reach precise agreement as to the logic of history; that is obvious. It is equally obvious that, if there be a Christian God at all, there must be a definite way in which he is related to the processes and development of society. This truth *is* the Christian philosophy of history, however partial and inadequate may be men's apprehensions of it. This is the truth we seek.

The subject takes on added importance when we realize that the present plight of civilization, as well as the present state of religion, is due in no small measure to neglect by the Church of its understanding of history. We pointed out in the preceding chapter that modern Christianity has presented God almost entirely as the Author of the cosmos and the Comforter of the individual human spirit, touching man in the outermost and inmost circles of his experience. It has had nothing to say of his relation to that sphere of life in which modern man has concentrated the great bulk of his energies and to which he has given devoted attention—the intermediate realm of social experience. In his social destiny, as we said, man is expected to work out his own salvation. The Social Gospel of modern religion has declared what we as Christians ought to do, not what God may or will do. And the result? Contemporary society, without insistent reminder of the divine conditions of social advance and of the divine retribution upon social profligacy, has driven it-

self deeper and deeper into the present morass of social chaos. The patent failure of the Church to blazon
that reminder vividly before the indifferent vision of
its society is another of the sins of apostasy for which it
must bow penitent.

It is important, also, to be clear that, in the Christian
message concerning society, three distinct questions are
involved, and that they are frequently confused. They
are:

1. What is the Christian *ideal* for society, the ultimate
goal toward which Christians should seek to make history
move?

2. What is the Christian *conviction* concerning the way
by which history develops? What, if any, are the factors,
especially cosmic factors, which condition the processes of
history, aiding or retarding society in its advance toward
the ultimate goal?

3. What is the Christian *program* in the face of the concrete issues of this moment of history? What is the Christian proposal for immediate social action?

Note that the modern Social Gospel has been almost
exclusively preoccupied with the first and the third
of these questions—discovering the Christian ideal for
society and then, in the light of that ideal, developing
detailed programs of social change. Here is the nub
of its inadequacy. For it is in the second question that
the Christian message concerning history comes to
focus; its answer to that question is the presupposition
of whatever else Christianity may have to say on so-

cial matters. For Christians, the one basic and central query is: How does the development of history occur? What, if any, are the forces in Ultimate Reality which surround and infuse the processes of human society and determine how they may or may not change? How do those forces wield their influence upon mankind's life? In brief, does God guide human society; and, if so, how?

With regard to the Christian *ideal* for society, the desirable goal of history, only two alternative views are possible. One declares that human history has no temporal goal on this planet; the final end is the gradual or cataclysmic dissolution of the present condemned world-order. If one accept this view, no further discussion of the matter is valuable. The alternative answer pictures the Christian objective as the slow and tedious, but progressive, approximation of an order of society completely expressive of Christian principles. With all allowance for diversity of vision as to details, the great outlines of this ideal order as Christians anticipate it are fairly clear. (1) It would guarantee fair and promising opportunities for life and livelihood to every person. In that very fundamental sense it would be an equilitarian and, I imagine, a 'classless' society. (2) It would be characterized by the absence of conflict between antagonistic groups, and by the presence of positive fellowship. It would be a co-operative com-

monwealth. (3) Its life in every aspect would be dominated by a universal apprehension of and devotion to
the highest values. It would, therefore, be a spiritual
society.

With so much agreement as to ideal goal, we come
to the main question. What is the Christian understanding of the way by which history advances? How
is God related to social processes? The answer is *the
Christian logic of history*. It is the attempt to discover
and define the controlling structure, if such there be,
within which human society moves.

To this question, three principal answers are being
given today:[5]

1. The first replies, *Man makes his own history*. So
flexible, so malleable, so undetermined are the underlying factors in mankind's corporate life that each succeeding generation very largely holds it within its
power to mould society to its chosen ideal. Evil men
may distort the human scene beyond possibility of re-
pair. By the same token, men of good will may make
history well, in the image of their hearts' desire.

Concerning God, this view is very vague. Like the
great astronomer, it has no need of him—at least as far
as society's welfare is concerned. If he be recognized at
all, he is thought of as standing somewhat apart from

[5] That there is a fourth, and truer, answer is the main contention of this
chapter.

the processes of history; and as severely limited, if not hopelessly handicapped, in the achievement of his purposes for mankind. Whatever their formal protestations of belief, those who give this answer actually recognize no operative influence of God upon society. In any event, God needs man's help. The issues of the better society and its realization within our finite world rest finally, if not entirely, upon man's effort. There are few stronger statements of this attitude than that of Josiah Royce:

"I don't ask so much who the Lord is, as what his will is. . . . God wants me to work; he asks service of me, not comprehension. . . . My philosophy consists in clear thinking about my duty; my faith is an assurance that the right will somehow conquer; my love is for those who desire God's kingdom to come; my hope is for the victory that is near at hand, and for the word, 'Well done, good and faithful servant!' The Lord needs me to help him against the mighty. . . . If he did not need me, my life would be vain." [6]

History presents no more attractive exemplar of this view than Royce's colleague, William James. You recall his famous declaration:

"If this life be not a real fight in which something is eternally gained for the universe by success, it is no better than a game of private theatricals from which one may withdraw at will. But it *feels* like a real fight—as if there

[6] Josiah Royce, *The Spirit of Modern Philosophy* (Houghton, Mifflin and Co.), p. 47. Needless to say, Royce is *not* here voicing his own conviction.

were something really wild in the universe which we are needed to redeem." [7]

This is the religion of the strenuous life, of moral effort, in which the whole destiny of the future hangs in the balance, and society's fate depends on man's loyalty. It is a *libertarian* view.

2. In the second view, *God alone rules history*. The rise and fall of society's health—all that happens—is illustrative of the steady, moulding determination of the judgment of God. This interpretation springs from a profound certainty of the continuous as well as the ultimate triumph of God's will. In religion, it breeds a tranquil saintly character rooted in lofty and joyous resignation before the inscrutable Providence of God—"the interest of the baffled and disappointed soul in coming into the presence of some external truth, some reality that is perfect, that lacks our weakness, that is victorious even though we fail, that is good even though we are worthless." [8]

We may scan the pages of history in vain for a nobler illustration of this attitude than Spinoza.

"Life has its wounds as well as its weapons. Your moral hero occasionally finds himself an outcast, as Spinoza was, who knows no army that will accept him, and who hears all human voices call him traitor. And then, indeed, he knows an experience that even the weaklings may aspire to

[7] William James, *The Will to Believe*, p. 61.
[8] Royce, *op. cit.*, p. 46.

share. He knows, namely, what it is to feel faint and sick at heart, and to see his own worthlessness. Then it occurs to him that perhaps the divine order, if haply it does really exist, may possibly need just his right arm a little less than he had thought. . . . After all, if there is a moral order, is it not complete unto itself? Did God wait all the eternities until I was ripened before he should triumph? Either he exists not at all—and then, how shall I create him?—or he exists, and then from eternity he has triumphed. His holiness I cannot create. Let me, if haply I may, see it, worship it, enjoy it as wondering, contemplative, adoring, helpless onlooker, consoled, if at all, by the knowledge that though I fail and am lost, he is from everlasting to everlasting." [9]

This is the philosophy of *determinism*.

3. There is a third answer. It suggests that the advance of human history from phase to phase is beyond the determinative control of either God or man. "Neither God nor we can do much about it." There *are* mighty hidden forces which underlie and, in the final outcome, determine the great sweeping changes in human society, both progress and retreat. But they are not agencies of the Divine. No more are they of human origin. They are—impersonal and inscrutable factors, of population, of economic law, of primitive impulse, or whatever—forces which are partly beyond human comprehension and certainly beyond human control. With equal certainty, they spring from no ethical source and they assure no ethical results. In a phrase which is gaining more and more currency in

[9] Royce, *op. cit.*, pp. 49–50.

our time, they are 'demonic' forces. In the last analysis this view is *fatalistic*.

Note that, from the religious interest, the first and third interpretations of history are closely akin. Each assumes that God is not in active and significant relationship to the social process. He does not guide the outcome of history.

Now, what is the present situation with regard to men's conviction in this matter? We need no reminder that it is the first of these three views—certainty of man's power to make the history of his own society— which has ruled the thought of the Modern Age. It is, I suspect, the wellnigh unanimous, if unspoken and unrecognized, assumption of the readers of these words —children of that Age. That *is* the surmise with which they actually contemplate their society and the possibilities for its progress. However, in the deeper insight of today, the libertarian interpretation is discredited along with the whole world-view of which it formed a part.

The contemporary scene discovers only one powerful spokesman of the second answer. Strictly speaking, the Marxist interpretation of history is of the second, not the first or third, type. It is rigidly deterministic. And, although it professes atheism, it affirms that history is in the grip of forces which are inexorably advancing society to higher and higher levels in the direction of an ideal goal. In other words, atheistic Communism is the only vigorous evangel of optimistic determinism claiming the convinced adherence of great numbers in the western world today. Here is suggestion of its power over the religiously minded. What an illustration of the condition of paradox which infests the current situation! And of the apostasy of religion's leadership to the Modern Age!

Now, one of the most significant facts about mankind's present predicament is the increasing permeation of men's inmost conviction by the third view of history—the supposition that the destiny of society is in the grip of forces which are neither divine nor human, but 'demonic.' Not consciously, to be sure, but tacitly, men are assuming that their present plight is the work of factors outside of earthly or heavenly control. And, more important, that the next stages in society's metamorphosis are beyond human power to influence, certainly beyond the power of those who might seek to mould history in the direction of God's purpose. For better or for worse, it is the 'demonic' philosophy which is increasingly ruling men's subconscious premises today. In the measure that it pervades conviction, it works the paralysis of effective social action.

It is this fact which gives final impetus to our search for the true Christian insight in this matter, what we have termed *the Christian logic of history*.

III

What can Christians definitely and confidently affirm concerning the nature of history?

I

First, *the ultimate outcome of history is within God's control.* This certainty is absolutely implicit in any Christian thought of God. To deny it, consciously or tacitly, is to have surrendered the Christian faith.

The Christian conviction in this matter is, historically, a direct legacy from the thought of the Old Testament prophets—that succession of strange, fantastic, almost fanatic figures who stand forth from the pages of history like great towering lighthouses—men who saw more deeply than their contemporaries the inner significance of what was transpiring before the eyes of all and who, straight in the face of prevailing opinion, kept confidently proclaiming coming events. To be sure, not all their predictions were fulfilled, especially in the precise manner they foretold. But, on the whole and in the large, their foresight was amazingly sound. At least they saw far more truly and dared to confront intractable fact far more courageously than any of their contemporaries. And the history of the succeeding centuries was not merely a judgment upon the peoples whose ways they condemned; it was a vindication of the insight of the Hebraic prophets, an in-

sight always characteristic of religion when faithful to
its inherent genius.[10] For, imbedded in their too limited thought of God as one who rules each particular
event for his immediate ends was the deeper truth
which is part of the Christian certainty in all ages—
that the flux of history in the large moves within conditions determined by fixed and immutable moral principles, the laws of God's ultimate Kingdom.

"Who hath measured the waters in the hollow of his
hand, and meted out heaven with the span, and compre-
hended the dust of the earth in a measure, and weighed
the mountains in scales, and the hills in a balance?

Who hath directed the Spirit of the Lord, or being his
counsellor hath taught him? . . .

Behold, the nations are as a drop of a bucket, and are
counted as the small dust of the balance: behold, he taketh
up the isles as a very little thing. . . .

All nations before him are as nothing; they are counted
to him less than nothing, and vanity. . . .

Have ye not known? have ye not heard? hath it not
been told you from the beginning? have ye not understood
from the foundations of the earth?

It is he that sitteth above the circle of the earth, and the
inhabitants thereof are as grasshoppers; that stretcheth out
the heavens as a curtain, and spreadeth them out as a tent
to dwell in;

That bringeth princes to nothing; he maketh the judges
of the earth as vanity. . . . And he shall also blow upon
them, and they shall wither, and the whirlwind shall take
them away as stubble." [11]

[10] On this, more below; see pp. 134 ff.
[11] Isaiah 40:12–24 (abridged). On the prophetic conviction, see especially George Adam Smith, *Isaiah*, Vol. I, Chaps. VI and VII.

THE MESSAGE IN SOCIETY'S CRISIS

The implacable judgments and flaming predictions of the prophets proceeded directly from their sure insight into the moral character of reality.

It was a central certainty of the prophets—God's reign in society. And, as we have already reminded ourselves, it was the conviction of the fathers of old. It is not necessary to go back to the dim origins of our faith for vivid illustration of this fact. We do not associate the name of Benjamin Franklin with flights of fancy or unthinking acquiescence in traditional sentiment. He once summarized a lifetime's reflection on the matter thus:

"I have lived, sir, a long time. And the longer I live, the more convincing proofs I see of this truth—that God governs in the affairs of men. And if a sparrow cannot fall to the ground without His notice, is it probable that an empire can rise without His aid? We have been assured, sir, in the sacred writings that except the Lord build the house, they labor in vain that build it. I firmly believe this; and I also believe that without His concurring aid we shall succeed in this political building no better than the builders of Babel; our projects will be confounded and we ourselves shall become a reproach and a byword down to future ages."

At the core of their belief, the fathers of old were not deceived. The truth of the matter is that human society does exist, grow and change within the encompassing, chastening, inexorable grip of the Rule of

God. This, I take it, is the foundation-stone of the Christian philosophy of history.

2

It is Christianity's profound certainty that the ultimate factors and forces which surround mankind's life in the large and determine its advance and retreat— the conditions of its true progress—are ethical in character. Indeed that economic forces or 'demonic' forces are, in the end of the day, determinative of human history in the measure that they are representative of moral realities and the instruments of moral purposes.[12] To the suggestion of the economic determination of history, or to the libertarian or the 'demonic' or the fatalistic view of history, Christianity proposes an alternative understanding—that of *the moral determination of history.*

By no means does this imply, as the thorough-going determinist insists, that each specific event in history occurs by God's deliberate act, or is completely harmonious with his designs. Far, far from it. Man's freedom to work *his* will upon the life of society and to bend its course out of the path of its highest destiny, God's intention for it, is great. So great, indeed, that

[12] From this, two corollaries follow. A true appraisal of these forces can be had only through understanding of the moral forces which condition and empower them. By the same token, wisdom for mankind's advance is to be sought primarily through deeper apprehension of the moral character of reality. See below, pp. 134–142.

there are times when the detection of any divine constraint whatever requires more insight than the passer-by can muster, more historic perspective than he possesses. The influence of God upon society's development is continuous, unwearying. But, like Nature's working, it is for the most part silent, stealthy, gentle, easily denied in its immediate effect. Only in the longer view is it readily discerned. I have elsewhere spoken of it as the 'moral structure of reality'—primordial and eternal principles which encompass the social life of mankind and determine the conditions of our human pilgrimage onward and upward.

Here the logic of the matter might have guided men's thoughts aright. For it must be obvious to the most untrained intelligence that, if there be a God at all, he must be One who is not only the Author of Nature and the Comforter of the solitary spirit, but One who has reserved to himself some measure of control over human society, its progress and its final destiny. He is the Governor of mankind's corporate life as well as the Friend of man's individual life. Not alone in the outermost and inmost circles of their experience, but in the intermediate circle as well, where they seek fortune, engage in combat and unleash the devastation of their vaulting ambition, must men confront the Sovereign of all Reality. Indeed, the contrary assumption—that the final determination of history's outcome, to make or to mar, lies within the power of human caprice—is a priori preposterous. It is a direct and ludicrous fruit of the Modern Mind's ego-centric perspective.

However, we are not dependent upon a priori probabilities in this matter. Christianity's conviction, like all profound certainties, is born of an initial intuition into the character of reality; but it receives abundant confirmation from fearless analysis of the brute facts of human history. If it be said that it is idealistic in content, it is an idealism made secure by the most determined and unremitting realism. The long story of mankind's pilgrimage is living demonstration of God in history. To eyes alert to discern its deeper significance, it reveals the constraint, the guidance, the impulsion of the moral structure of reality, the principles of the Divine Commonwealth.

3

God's influence upon society is most easily discerned as judgment and as discipline. Especially is this true in epochs of social cataclysm and disintegration. So we discern it today.

Speaking to students upon the most unpopular of texts, "The wages of sin is death," one of our ablest college preachers is fond of chiding them that they do not believe it true only because they have not put it to a sufficiently thorough-going test. His message runs somewhat as follows: "Stop being dilettante in your sins. Come on now. Sin! Really *sin!* SIN—gloriously, determinedly, undiscourageably! And, before very long, you will find yourself in a box six feet long by two feet wide by two feet high." To prove the text true, one need only sin with sufficient abandon, imagination and dogged determination. This is obvious enough in personal experience. It is Christianity's insight that it is no less true for society. As with the individual, it is possible to misuse the opportunities of freedom and wander from the course of sound progress. But only a certain distance. Then the constraining tension of the moral structure of reality makes itself felt, as corrective and as punishment. Just as a too flagrant defiance of the laws of health brings its inevitable penalty in sickness or death, so any generation or nation or community which violates the laws of social wellbeing and progress too persistently or too jubilantly does so to its own destruction. The fate of one after another of the great empires, the disintegration and disappearance of one civilization after another, is history's testimony to the soundness of religion's insight. The wages of sin *is* death. And these wages are paid with the fidelity and impersonality of an automatic paymaster. The Christian is assured of the implacability of the judgment of God upon society's life. His is a sound apprehension of the great immutable moral structures which furnish the framework of society's as of each man's life. Without them no order, no progress would be possible; but by the same token they bring their inevitable penalty upon the ruthless or wilful, or even the careless, violator. This is the element of determinism in all profoundly religious world-views.

There is a deeper aspect of this truth. It has frequently been pointed out that, in human experience, there is no such thing as a 'return to barbarism.' What is so described is always a descent to something-worse-than-barbarism. The monkey who behaves as a monkey is natural and amusing, or perhaps pathetic. The man who behaves as a monkey is degenerate and tragic. A child who has once glimpsed the dignity of manhood's self-determination can never return to childhood's irresponsibility; his lapse to childish ways is always a descent to lower than the child's estate. A man who has once risen above slavery to selfishness and egotism in response to the claims of high devotion never returns to his old selfish life; he falls to an existence lower and cheaper than his former self. The race which has climbed from primitivism to some apprehension of civilized society never 'relapses' to its former barbarism, but to a condition which is sub-barbaric. A generation which has caught a clear vision of a higher ordering of corporate life cannot desert that vision and give itself once again to its old loves; it may desert the vision, but in so doing it wills its own decay. More specifically, the generation which had clearly envisioned the abolition of human slavery could not return to their parents' easy acquiescence in the practice; such acquiescence would have been, for them, moral decline. A generation which has had held before its imagination the possibility of a united and warless world and has pledged its allegiance to that ideal, cannot return to the old order. It may resume the old ways; but it is actually condemning itself to retrogression, to a lower state of civilization, to the threat of mortal disintegration. This is the issue in the fate of our society. My grandfather might be held blameworthy for murder. But my father, for hate. And I, for 'all uncharitableness.' Our fathers' mistakes are, in us, sin. But our fathers' sins are, in us, degeneracy. In each instance, the final state is not a repetition of the first, but its perversion. The end is not a 'recovery of normalcy,' but decadence. And decadence, unless it be overtaken and radically redeemed, is the precursor of death. This is the obverse of the promise of all moral advance.

Here is an obdurate law of our human experience, both personal and corporate. It is clear evidence of the 'moral structure of reality.' It is final refutation of all 'cyclic' interpretations of human history. And it is glorious proof of Nature's purpose to progress. Our human lot, both individual and corporate, is a pilgrimage—a pilgrimage forward and upward. Reality will have no slackers and no turncoats. We must go higher, or we *shall* go lower.

In this view, the ultimate explanation of the present world confusion and chaos is in terms of inevitable retribution for the selfishness and sin of society's recent practice—wilful or careless blindness to the moral structure of reality. These are not the sole causes of our travail; mistakes due to unavoidable ignorance and the blundering which accompanies all man's stumbling advance have had their part. But selfishness and sin are the root causes, the key causes. They are the fulcrum of the problem—where men knew better and might have done better and are blameworthy for the tragic outcome. If I may be permitted to repeat what I have written elsewhere,[13] "The world's present agony is the judgment of history upon our life. It is a revelation of the moral order of the universe, of what earlier generations would have preferred to call the Will of God. It is history's stern reminder that we live in a world where material and selfish ideals cannot finally prevail, that ethical considerations in some sense underlie and precede and determine economic and political problems, that our corporate existence does move within the constraining framework of the moral design of God. For nation, for community, for epoch, as for individual, the wages of sin is death."

Many, I know, will recoil from so forbidding an

[13] *The Plain Man Seeks for God*, p. 121.

interpretation. I seem to hear more than one voice raised in protest: "Surely you have the matter all out of proportion. People today are weary enough without having the righteousness of God trumpeted above their heads. We confront a generation baffled, confused, discouraged, exhausted. What it seeks and deserves is comfort not condemnation, reassurance not reproof, encouragement not the Wrath of God. You have given us the message of the Old Testament. The New Testament declares to men a God of Love and Strength and Hope. Give us the God of Jesus."

On the contrary, to fail to give the Christian conviction concerning history in some such terms as have been suggested is to be traitorous to a central element in the Christian faith. The loving Father of Jesus' experience is not a substitute for the God of the prophets, but his completion. He is the fuller portrait of the indignant ruler of Amos' and Micah's and Isaiah's scorching judgments. And in the fuller portrayal, all the authentic lineaments of their true vision are assumed and reappear. Indeed, only through obedience to the Moral Sovereign of the world's life may one rise to secure certainty of the solicitous Father of Love. This appears to have been Jesus' own conviction: "If they will not listen to Moses and the prophets, how shall they believe though one rose from the dead?" Our generation is exactly like an invalid suffering from a malignant growth and guzzling patent medicines to cure the ills enumerated on the labels, when a major operation is indicated. It is the Church's responsibility to be the spiritual physician for society, to seek to diagnose its ills and prescribe for their cure. Its duty is to tell the patient the truth, not what he wishes to believe true.

The truth is there has been sin in our society—not 'social sin' for society cannot do wrong, but individual sin with profound social consequences—"the sin of gluttony for money and for power and for a specious prosperity; the sin of sharp and heartless business practice, of false objectives, of unlimited reliance upon basically unethical axioms; the sin of blindness which could not see the truth because it did not love the right—such sin as exacts its wage not merely from the sinners but from their fellowmen." It is often said that the Depression and its accompanying problems are due to the complexity of modern civilization, a complexity which no man can comprehend and for which no man is to blame; that they have resulted from ignorance, from unavoidable mistake. All that is but very partially true. It will not do to plead ignorance, unavoidable mistake. When a man carelessly sets fire to his neighbor's house, we do not excuse his ignorance; adults are expected to know that fire destroys. When a man deliberately looses germs upon a community, we do not speak of unavoidable mistake; we know the havoc of disease. But the laws of society's health are written almost as plainly across the pages of history as the laws of Nature or the laws of physical health. And they are written in the words of the spiritual seers of mankind, supremely in the mind of him whom Christians call Master.[14] If we were to summarize the major cause of our present trials, bluntly but fully within the facts, it would be: our generation, its accepted business and political leaders who have set the pace and its rank and file who have jubilantly followed their example, you and I, have been flaunting the underlying moral principles for society's health— gloriously, determinedly, undiscourageably. We are paying, and shall pay, the cost—unto the third and fourth generation.

We have cited the most familiar and contemporary evidence. It is only the most vivid, because most recent, illustration of the truth to which all human history bears abundant testimony. The Christian is confirmed in his insight that the ultimately determinative conditions of human history *are* ethical and that they will finally prevail.

14 Lest it be charged that this argument is left wholly in generalities, let me cite three fundamental and obvious laws of economic health, each of which was deliberately and persistently flaunted by the business leaders of this nation in the last decade. You cannot continue expansion indefinitely in the face of disappearing foreign markets. You cannot continue to lend to a debtor who has no means of repayment. You cannot burn up 20,000,000 lives, not to speak of unmeasured material wealth without paying the price in lowered standards of living. Yet the avowed business policy of our national leaders and of the great majority of our citizens was set in direct defiance of these three simple and patent principles. I believe that every banker and businessman and politician and citizen who joined in these practices bears personal guilt for the present suffering of millions.

4

By the same token and from precisely the same sources of insight, the Christian understanding of history declares *the only ways by which social ills can be soundly and permanently rectified*. It dictates the conditions of effective social change, the methods in the social struggle to which Christians can give ready support. It is implicit in Christianity's certainty of the ethical unity of reality that it places confidence in no methods for the accomplishment of social change—however worthy the goal—which are not themselves consonant with the goal desired. The end cannot justify the means. To employ injustice, violence, ruthless coercion for the achievement of socially desirable ends is to set loose in the world forces of evil which—the universe being a moral organism—are certain to take their toll from those who employ them and to qualify, and in some measure nullify, the good ends achieved. Any measures which shall rebuild society closer to the vision of the ideal must themselves be consistent with that ideal.

Here, again, while the Christian conviction rises in the first instance from its own intuition of the moral character of reality, it receives abundant confirmation from an objective scrutiny of human history itself. The train of tragic consequences which succeeded the

American Civil War is a vivid case in point. How much more the hound-pack of ills which the Great War loosed and which still dog our heels today! How far Christians may find themselves compelled to the use of milder forms of coercion under what appear to be the necessities of social conflict is a very puzzling question. That they cannot lend acquiescence to the types and extent of coercion which are avowed by many of the social programs of the day seems indisputable. Above all, Christians cannot link their own program for social regeneration with a philosophy of method alien to their ethical consciousness.[15]

The Christian is not entitled to the same measure of self-deception in these matters as may be excused in others. He cannot persuade himself that all opponents of change, the defenders of the *status quo,* are evil men —dominated wholly by lust for power and aggrandizement. He cannot pretend that his own motives are unmixed, unless they are continually purged by the testing catharsis of inner purity. He cannot identify a specific immediate social advance with the Kingdom of God; he should know better than that. He cannot deceive himself that the end justifies the means; the very pith of his faith denies it.

Christianity has watched the rise and fall of empire after empire, civilization after civilization. It has seen

---

[15] Here, I take it, lies one point of irreconcilable conflict between Christianity and the program of Communism. See below, pp. 159 ff.

economy succeed economy, each trusting in some particular economic or political dogma, each proclaiming the final significance of its proposals, each refusing adequate recognition to the ethical considerations which alone could have given it power to endure. Christianity has witnessed its own movement persisting through the advent and decline of system after system. More important, it knows that the vigor and significance of its endurance in any agony of transition were proportionate to its disentanglement from the unethical economic and political dogmas then prevailing, its fidelity to its faith in the moral character of reality. It sees no reason to expect that in our day programs based largely on non-ethical premises and employing non-ethical means for their triumph will achieve greater permanence or bring greater benefit to mankind.

If the Kingdom of Heaven is to be securely built within our society, it must be constructed from materials and by methods of its own nature. They, too, must be ethical.

5

We have stressed the element of judgment in God's impact upon society. Is that the last word? I think not. Just as this is only one side of the Christian view of personal life, so it is only one aspect of the Christian understanding of history. There is judgment in the flux of history. So, also, there is redemption.

Certainly this is true of the Christian faith concerning human nature—a faith confirmed times without number in the marvel of redemption. The wages of sin *is* death. And, as we have said, these wages are paid with the fidelity and impersonality of an automatic paymaster. But the marvel of personal redemption has about it nothing of the impersonal, the mechanical, the inscrutable. Very quietly, very simply, the inner life of the individual can be transformed, drastically, radically, sometimes immediately, in a way which no mere understanding of judgment could possibly anticipate or explain. This is a central paradox of God's way with men—the implacability of judgment, but the infinite flexibility and possibility of redemption. Here is the crucial question. Is it possible to draw any analogy from redemption in individual souls to the life of society, as we have noted parallels between the punitive consequences of personal wrongdoing and similar effects of social evil? If the miracle of grace may enter a life seemingly condemned to tragic fate and reclaim it to self-control, to power, to great usefulness, is it possible for the same influence to work its way in society? This is the query on which Christians who are deeply concerned for the succor of our sick and chastened and impotent civilization should fasten their attention.

Here, our light is far more flickering. However, we do detect the redemptive purposes of God effecting their ends within society's life, in every age and in our own time. And in at least two ways.

a. First, in the moulding, building, healing processes which underlie and undergird all social progress. These may, in some measure, be likened to the silent but ever-active healing and nourishing processes of physical life which are forever overtaking the ravages of disease, nurturing health and furthering growth. We saw evidence of this in the law that no man or race returns to old and lower ways, but always to something far worse than the previous level. We must go higher or we shall go lower. We noted the law in its sombre aspect of discipline. But, like all laws of true moral discipline, it is in reality a law of progress. It is the beneficent structure of an experience which intends that men shall achieve. The immediate issues of history which press upon our gaze and screen from our vision the farther perspectives and higher vistas may lower dark and threatening. The longer view suggests unmistakably the outlines of tedious and faltering but sure advance. On the mooted question of human progress, this much seems clear: we approximate the ideal of absolute perfection no closer than our fathers, partly because the passions which subdued them still rise in our breasts to bring us to defeat and shame, and partly because with each successive generation's achievement there are revealed hitherto undiscovered possibilities claiming yet more exacting effort. But there is advance, the attainment of new heights from which the still higher ranges are disclosed. We have no slightest ground for condescension toward those who have gone the way of life before us. We *are* entitled to take courage that the pilgrimage of our race is no disguised treadmill, but a plodding advance into an inexhaustible Beyond. To our view there appear to be tragic and irredeemable regressions. They are temporary setbacks. Intractable obstacles, whether individuals or nations or whole civilizations, crumble and dissolve. The irresistible currents sweep slowly past and on. This much at least of the divine intention for mankind unfailingly achieves realization—through the passage of the ages, the race does go forward.

In this light, the judgment of God upon society appears as intended not primarily for punishment, but for redemption. It is the flushing away of cluttered refuse which must precede any sound advance. It is the laborious scraping of barnacles from the hull which must take place if the Ship of State is to cleave the waves with safety and power. It is the excision of diseased parts by a major operation which is the precondition for healthy growth. Severe and cruel in its impact upon individuals and groups, this purging process appears. Whole nations and peoples and generations seem to be swept aside and humiliated. Painful it undoubtedly is, and dangerous—as dangerous as a major operation. *And* as necessary, when acute infection has rendered any other measure futile. In the long sweep of history's ages it is seen to be necessary. And it is seen to be fruitful. It is an inevitable and inexorable feature of moral reality, a condition of mankind's social advance and of the realization of God's good purpose for society. Its outcome is redemptive.

Walter Horton likens this double process by which the divine influence moves in history, through judgment and through redemption, to two hands of God.

"Is it tenable, one may ask, that God should be at once a God of wrath and a God of love? Has He two hands, one iron-gloved, the other warm and human? Is it conceivable that He should alternately woo us with the one and strike us with the other? Could we believe this, we might perhaps hear Him saying to our generation, in tones of mingled sorrow and anger, 'You must and shall have deeper fellowship in your social order. You may take it *this* way (stretching out the right hand) or you may take it *this* way (clenching the left fist). If you will hear my Word, you may make the great soulless machine of your industrial civilization an instrument for the common good and a bond of fellowship between you; but if not, then I will smash your civilization, and reduce you to a more primitive level of existence where you *must* recover the art of fellowship, which your pioneering forefathers knew and you have lost.'" [16]

b. However, it is not only, or mainly, through the imperceptible and impersonal forces which undergird

[16] Walter M. Horton, *Realistic Theology* (Harper & Brothers), p. 112.

the stream of history that God's redemptive purpose for mankind is wrought. It is *in* individual persons one by one that the miracle of redemption most vividly appears. It is *through* such individuals, thus redeemed, that the same redemptive influence finds entrance into the tattered and powerless body of society.

This is the clear teaching of history. In every age, and most significantly in times of retrogression and despair, have appeared men and women through whose vision and will the tides of history have been reversed, retreat has been turned into advance, man's life has been thrust forward to new and higher levels. No uninspired view could possibly have anticipated their advent. No merely naturalistic explanation could possibly account for their emergence. In no sense are they children of their age, except as the decadence of their age has bred in them revulsion from its every feature and indomitable determination radically to transform its inner being. The redemptive power which courses through them most spectacularly is, in less tragic moments, forever quietly at its winnowing and healing and hallowing work through men and women of their fellowship.[17]

"Two great superhuman processes seem to run through history: a grim process of action and reaction, in which the proud and cruel are usually victorious, and then meet Nemesis by over-reaching themselves; and a quiet mysteri-

[17] See further, below, pp. 144–146.

ous process of assimilation wherein the men of God win their way, against appalling obstacles, by soul-force alone. Neither of these processes guarantees the inevitability of Progress, since the former is purely negative and defensive, so to speak, and the latter is perpetually defeated by those who despise and reject the importunities of the Spirit; yet this much can be said with assurance, that we live in a world where the triumph of evil can never be complete, since evil systems eventually destroy themselves by their own greed and egotism, and the Spirit is never more persuasive than when it suffers silently, unflinchingly, beneath the heel of oppression. Against the stonewall defensive structure of God's elemental justice, earth's conquerors and exploiters hurl themselves eventually to their own destruction; against the power of God's forgiving love and grace, the hearts of evil men are never so fast-locked but that they may be captured by some sudden surprise attack." [18]

Comprehension of this fact is Christianity's second distinctive contribution to the philosophy of history. Like the vision of the moral character of reality, it sets Christianity at enmity with all rigidly deterministic or fatalistic or 'demonic' interpretations of history. Their temptation is to fasten attention upon general tendencies, the play of great impersonal and uncontrollable forces, and to read history in these terms, mechanistically. So, their conclusions appear fatalistic and pessimistic. The outcome is a gloomy one. We recoil from their despair; but we cannot put our finger on their inadequacy. They falsify the story because they

[18] Horton, *op. cit.*, pp. 112-113.

have lost from their view *the recreative principle in history*—the vision of life and influence of the individual person. We speak of the Christian ideal as a 'society dominated by love.' That is not altogether accurate. It, again, speaks of an abstraction. Rather, the Christian ideal is a society permeated, and in some measure redeemed, by the influence of loving persons. In that ideal is revealed the force upon which Christianity chiefly relies for the gradual emancipation and improvement of society.

Now we see the focus of the Christian hope for society. It is in and through men and women who have caught some vision of God's hope for his world, have come to some understanding of the laws of his moral governance without which that hope may not be realized, and are possessed by a passionate will to be used by him for its realization. They are the principal agencies of God's redemption for mankind.

Thus we are brought to our final topic—the contributions of personal religion to social salvation. But, first, one further and related element in the Christian logic of history must be recorded—the twofold strategy of Christianity in its social mission.

6

The Christian view of history must always remind itself of the three distinct spheres in which each man's existence moves. In all the ebb and flow of society, the

marks of vital personal religion whenever it has been true and powerful. Its gift to society's problems is not merely, as is so often said, character which shall follow and utilize knowledge, directing it to high purposes; but, also, a truer comprehension of the facts themselves, greater knowledge.

We should know this, we who claim to stand in the succession of the Old Testament prophets. It is easy to say that the historical insight of the prophets was a reasoned inference or deduction from their view of God and God's relation to mankind. It is a quite misleading statement of the matter. They would never have recognized such an account as true. Rather, their amazing interpretations of the meaning of passing events and the inevitable outcome in the future were immediate certainties in reaction to the brute facts of contemporary history—like sparks flashed from the impact of glancing metal on tempered steel. They were no conscious deductions from rational convictions about God; they were direct insights made possible through a vivid interior awareness of God. In brief, they sprang directly from the heart of their inner life.

The amazing prescience which they brought to their age should be part of their successors' equipment today.

"To see the truth and tell it, to be accurate and brave about the moral facts of our day—to this extent the Vision and the Voice are possible for every one of us. . . . Let us remember that to see facts as they are and to tell the truth about them—this also is prophecy."[21]

We repeat—there should proceed from the life of religion, understanding of contemporary history and wisdom for the guidance of events.

Precisely how religion's gift of insight is derived, it is not easy to declare. Certainly it is not by adding information, facts. Partly it proceeds from the possession of a broader and clearer perspective. The inner experience of religion should lift one up from the swirling stream of history where sound judgment is impossible, to a place of relative quiet and of higher vantage ground; there one may survey the fast-flowing flux with some detachment; there one may bring the powers of a steady and unbiased mind to bear upon its meaning; there one may open a receptive consciousness to the imprint of its significance; and thereby one may perceive more truly and judge more competently. Hocking has well said:

"That which chiefly marks the religious soul is a fearless and original valuation of things. Its judgments emerge somehow from solitude, as if it had resources and data of its own, sufficient to determine its attitudes without appeal to the bystander, as if by fresh contact with truth itself, it were sure of its own justice."[22]

[21] On this whole matter of prophetic insight, see George Adam Smith, *The Book of the Twelve Prophets*, Vol. I, pp. 81–88.
[22] W. E. Hocking, *The Meaning of God in Human Experience*, p. 28.

There is much talk today about fleeing to personal religion for escape from life. But there is a rising to personal religion for a truer view of life, that one may return into the maelstrom of life with some gift of criticism, of wisdom, of prophecy.

Nevertheless, this is not the whole secret of religion's insight. There is a deeper issue here. It lies in the baffling but vitally important question of the relation of character to understanding, even political and social and economic understanding. Religion yields wisdom not by adding to our information, but by furnishing a perspective where that information may be truly seen, and then by supplying norms through which that information may be rightly appraised, by sensitizing and training our latent intuitive sense for the value of facts and the meaning of events. All supremely important truth is truth of value. Not least, economic and social and political truths, affecting as they do the intimate destinies of mankind's millions. Such truth can be rightly understood only in the light of its ethical significance. There are prerequisites to its sound comprehension and appraisal. They are prerequisites akin to the truth itself—prerequisites of ethical sensitivity, of moral character.

This contention will not readily be accepted. Or, if it is, it will be a perfunctory assent which is belied by our working assumptions. We simply do not believe it today. The amazing grasp of history, the astounding foresight of the Old Testament prophets, we find it difficult to explain. But, after all, they lived centuries ago and in a relatively simple economy. Personal religion may have given them some insight; their prophecy may have been good luck. In any event, ours is a different world, and ours are different problems. We live in a civilization so intricate, so complex, that only those of distinctive intellectual gifts, special training and elaborate information can possibly understand it and diagnose its ills. This is no task for the personal religionist, but for the economist, the financier, the statesman. Knowledge, skill, education—they are the conditions of insight.

Are they? One would think that the lamentable failure of national leadership during the past few years were sufficient refutation. Let us illustrate our query from one bitter episode in recent national experience. It is an aspect of the painful development of the Depression which has been too little noted. These are the main facts, familiar to us all:

In the autumn of 1929 began a crumbling of the business and financial structure of the nation which reached a temporary climax in the stock market crash of October and November of that year. It had been foreseen for many months by far-visioned observers in this and other lands. The most courageous had not hesitated to predict its advent, and its probable serious proportions. Not a few economic novices had foreseen it, knowing in their bones that our excessive inflation was unsound, that the much-heralded prosperity of the nation was exaggerated and that our self-delusion could not be permanently maintained. Nevertheless, to most Americans, it came as a terrifying shock. We all recall that when the crash fell, President Hoover summoned to Washington successive groups of leaders from every walk of national life—governors of states, bankers, industrialists, economists, lawyers, college presidents and so forth. Do you also remember that under his leadership, each one of those groups issued a unanimous public statement? The statements were essentially identical; their substance was—that the then existing depression was temporary and largely psychological, that the fundamental business structure of the country was sound, and that if only we got busily at work and told one another that all was well, within a very brief time —six months at most—the country would be back in its normal health and prosperity. Most of us gladly accepted their comforting assurances.

What did the turn of events prove? Within twelve months, between ten and sixteen million of our workers were unemployed. Bread lines and relief drives were familiar incidents of daily life. Our more thoughtful leaders were questioning whether the fundamental economic structure of the nation had not been proven unsound and might not have to be overhauled. A wave of increasing pessimism was sweeping over the minds of the people. The nation was caught in the grip of the most crippling business crisis of modern times.

There is only one phase of that story to which I invite attention. How are we to account for the disparity between the confident predictions of the most intelligent, best educated, best trained, best informed men in the nation and the actual development of events? Three obvious explanations suggest themselves at once:

1: We may say it was the failure of *ignorance*. Our leaders did not and could not foresee what would occur; no one could have known what was coming. But that is to impute to them a lack of intelligence which is not credible. There were others, less intelligent, less well informed, who foresaw the outcome clearly and foretold it; though few.

2: It might be suggested that it was a failure of *character*—that they knew well enough the probable turn of events but deliberately told untruth in order to save their reputations. This explanation is unthinkable.

3: It might be attributed to a failure of *judgment*. Our leaders foresaw what was coming, but feared to alarm people unduly and so falsified their own expectations in the hope that some kindly Providence would intervene and avert the impending disaster. But their own disclaimers preclude this explanation. Even if it were sound, we still would have to account for so lamentable an error of judgment in men so able and so well informed.

140

4: Is it possible that there is a fourth explanation which comes closer to the truth? Is it possible that they failed—that we *all* failed—to foresee the dangers threatening the life of our people, because we were not sufficiently devoted to the truth—sufficiently determined to know the truth however unpleasant and at whatever cost to our pride, our biases, and our hopes, to be able to foresee what must occur? Is it possible that we are here at the most difficult and delicate point in the whole range of human life—the point where ethical devotion actually quickens insight, and quickened insight controls action; the problem of responsibility for truth which a man did not consciously see, but which he might have seen, and because he might have, should have seen? Our failure—the failure from which millions of our countrymen are suffering—was a failure in devotion to truth, a failure in *attunement of the inner life*.

If "the ultimate factors and forces which surround mankind's life in the large and determine its advance and retreat—the conditions of its true progress—are ethical in character" and "economic forces are determinative of human history only in the measure that they are representative of moral realities," then a true appraisal of their significance can be had only through understanding the moral forces which condition and empower them. By the same token, wisdom for mankind's advance is to be sought primarily through deeper apprehension of the moral character of reality. It is a gift of personal religion.

3

Vision of the ideal; insight into the actual. *Religion's radicalism* is born of this double parentage. For true Christianity is incurably, indomitably radical—radical in its relentless exposure of the inadequacies, the brutalities, the stupidities of the prevailing order; radical in its restless and unappeasable dissatisfaction with things as they are; radical in its unwearying struggle for change—drastic, fundamental, ultimately revolutionary change; radical in its life-devotion to an ideal for society which human eyes shall never see fully realized, its faith that that ideal may be made real. This is not to say that all religious radicals are wise or fully Christian in their radicalism. It is to say that all true Christians are, in a profound sense, necessarily radical. That is the conclusion of Professor Hocking's masterly inquiry into the actual influence of religion in history: "From such a survey but one uncontradicted impression emerges: the thing has been radical." [23]

Partly, religion's radicalism is due to the fact that it has seen the ideal and knows it to be practicable. Knows it not merely because religion has caught a fleet-

[23] W. E. Hocking, *op. cit.,* pp. 11-12.

ing and imaginary glimpse of it, but because it has actually *experienced* the ideal as real, has grasped it—fragmentarily and partially to be sure, but none the less truly—within its inmost experience and has found it real. For religion is, as Hocking again says, "anticipated attainment—the present attainment in a single experience of those objects which in the course of nature are reached only at the end of infinite progression." [24] It is not merely vision of the ideal; it is possession of the ideal. Its final word is not, "I hope, I wish, I long"; but "I know." The Kingdom of Heaven is within. No wonder religion's devotion to the ideal is dauntless and undiscourageable.

On the other hand, religion's radicalism is due partly to the fact that it has seen more incisively, more sensitively, more profoundly into the facts of contemporary existence, things as they actually are. And, in the light of the possible, it knows them to be intolerable. Its very solitariness, the fact that it stands somewhat apart from the pressure of immediacy and from the corporate will's insistence on conformity, enables it to see society in far truer perspective. It cannot be blind to the cruel, the stupid, the unjust features of our present social and national life. Just as it cannot tolerate in itself subtle dishonesties, meannesses, cruelties which pass easily enough in the muddied standards of the mass; so it cannot tolerate in its society the blindnesses and in-

[24] *Op. cit.*, p. 31.

justices of the prevailing order. It knows them to be unnecessary. It knows them to be wrong. Yes, and it also knows them to be ultimately destructive of society itself. It is as though two mirrors were held before the eyes of the inner life, the one revealing society precisely as it is, the other as in all truth it might be. From the contrast of those pictures, as from the coming together of a positive and negative pole of electricity, there bursts a flame of passion and devotion—religion's incurable radicalism.

Furthermore, it is a radicalism not of talk only—an effervescent and evanescent enthusiasm, comprised largely of condemnation of corporate sin, especially other men's sins. It is a radicalism of action. Forth from the Christian movement in the nineteen centuries of its history has come a succession of powerful movements for the liberation and amelioration of mankind.

Hocking, in the investigation of the nature of religion just quoted, speaks of the distinctive function of religion as that of 'perpetual parentage.' History discovers it as 'the mother of the arts.' "All the arts of common life owe their present status and vitality to some sojourn within the historic body of religion; there is little in what we call culture which has not at some time been a purely religious function." [25] It has borne one after another of the arts—not only music and painting and sculpture and drama and architecture, but also

[25] Hocking, *op. cit.*, p. 13.

144

dancing, legislation, science, philosophy, moral control; has given them birth and has nurtured them through their critical infancy. Then, as they have attained maturity and sufficient strength to exist in independence, religion has sent them forth to continue their development as secular enterprises—often not without the struggle and hard-feeling so characteristic of adolescence's break from home.

Religion has performed the same function of parentage for almost every great enterprise for human improvement in the Christian centuries. Hospitals, schools and colleges, institutions for the unfortunate and the outcast, general philanthropy—*all* had their birth within the life of the Church. All were maintained there under religion's guardianship and at religion's expense until they were vigorous enough to stand alone and the public conscience could be educated to their maintenance.

Yes, but religion has been not only the mother of the arts and the sponsor of the philanthropies. It has been the father of the prophets. And of their successive crusades for human liberation. Name over the great reform movements of the Christian era—for abolition of the slave-trade, for prison-reform, for abolition of slavery itself, for improved conditions of labor, for protection of women and children, for slum clearance, for temperance, for world-peace—without exception each at its inception a daring and dangerous crusade in the face of then-prevailing sentiment; each pioneered by men and women directly under Christian impulse, many of them born and nurtured at the heart of the life of the Church.[26] This is the reply of history to the charge of the social ineffectiveness of religion. If it be true that, in our times, great movements for human emancipation have come to birth without the fructification of religion, it is, with the possible exception of the French Revolution, almost the first time it has occurred in the Christian centuries. There is matter for reflection here.

If our contemporary religion has ceased to thrust forth into the life of society great and ever-new crusades for reform, it does not mean that religion has no significant contribution for social life. It is proof of the senility of contemporary Christianity. For religion is not merely vision of the ideal; it is love of the ideal—such love and loyalty as breed lifelong devotion. It commands action. Religion begins in the conviction that what *should* be, *can* be; it continues, tireless and indomitable, in the determination that what *can* be, *shall* be.

4

Thus, we come at the end to a final gift of religion to social effectiveness. If we speak of it last, it is ap-

---

26 *Cf.* for example *Christian Social Reformers of the Nineteenth Century*, edited by Hugh Martin, a collection of brief biographies of the great British reformers from John Howard to Keir Hardie who pioneered the transformation of English social life in the last century.

propriately, because it is climactic, the most important contribution of all. If we speak of it briefly, it is because it is so obvious. It is Fidelity, the particular quality of religion's devotion to ideals. Or in religion's own vocabulary—FAITH.

"Faith," however, is one of the weather-worn words of religion—a term of a thousand meanings and, for many, of hackneyed associations. One thinks at once of the lad who replied to his Sunday School questionnaire that "faith is believing what you know ain't true." In one of its aspects, faith *is* confidence in convictions which are believed to be true but which are never fully proven true. But in another of its aspects, faith is life-devotion to ideals which are felt to be sound and which are believed to be achievable, but which are never completely achieved.

> "Think not the faith by which the just shall live,
> Is a dead creed, a map correct of heaven,
> Far less a feeling fond and fugitive,
> A thoughtless gift, withdrawn as soon as given.
> It is an affirmation and an act
> That bids eternal truth be present fact." [27]

The importance of such a temper at the core of the life of those who are going out into the times which lie just ahead should be clear enough. If one were asked what it is which these times will most urgently need, the answer would be unhesitating—*men and*

[27] Hartley Coleridge.

147

women with sticking power. The final outcome of the cataclysmic changes which are shaking the world's life almost every hour and challenging every cherished assumption of our forebears, it is impossible to predict. The precise form which the Christian message to a new age should take, we cannot foresee. One thing we know—we are moving into a day which will tax to the last limit both the wisdom and the endurance of every idealist.

Many of us received our tutelage in the social significance of Christianity in a time of roseate optimism. We took with dead seriousness the ideals of Mr. Wilson. We believed it was a War which would end war, to make civilization safe for democratic society. We actually expected—within our lifetime—to see the abolition of war, to accomplish racial reconciliation, to build a new industrial order, a more Christian society. What a vaporous mirage those expectations now seem, the daydreams of an almost forgotten childhood! We shall never see that fairer earth in our lifetime. It is no part of Christian realism to pretend that we shall. It is a life-job we are enlisted in; and in every aspect of the Christian ideal for society. There is no place in it for those who are not prepared to endure to the end. We stand fully in the succession of the men of old who 'saw afar the shining city of God and left the service of the commonplace in devotion to their vision'; but who also 'died in faith, not having received the promises, but having seen them afar off.' The need today is for men of faith.

By no means is this to suggest that only those whose inner lives are fed from the springs of personal religion are capable of such endurance. The long procession of secular reformers who, in poverty, in persecution and in defeat, have held their ground immovable is sufficient refutation of such absurd pretension. One thinks at once of Voltaire, of Eugene V. Debs, of Karl Marx, and of many a comrade in this and earlier ages. *It is the peculiar form of devotion which should characterize Christians* which the inner life must sustain—dogged, unremitting striving, joined with patience, fairness, forgiveness, steadiness, optimism, hope—the temper of faith.

How such enduring devotion is formed in the inner life, it is not difficult to state. Exhausted with fruitless struggle, we retire to its friendly comfort, there to have our wounds dressed, our spirits relaxed and rested, our famished souls replenished. It may be a haven of escape; but it should be the agent of rehabilitation without which we cannot continue in vigor and power. Rebuffed and retreating, we climb again to its point of vantage to survey the scene afresh, to re-examine our strategy lest it have been faulty, and then to give ourselves to new measures, or to old measures with strengthened conviction. It may be the easy refuge of the spectator; but it should be the means of correction without which we may spend our energies in misdirected and futile wastage. Harried by misunderstanding, cruel misrepresentation and brutal opposition, we seek its quiet peace to regain poise and patience and good humor. It may encourage weak rationalization; but it should provide that purification without which most of us cannot crusade as Christians. Flushed and jubilant with victory, we pause in its calm to give thanks, to repent any unkindness, to steady our minds and hearts for the next advance. It may gratify self-congratulation; it should hallow life's great satisfactions. Discouraged near to despair or tempted almost beyond resistance to some cheap short-cut, we enter once more into the inmost chambers of the soul—there to reclaim afresh our vision of the ideal, to have renewed within us our experience of its reality, and so again to be made certain that devotion to it is alone worth life's all. It may be the nurse of all manner of self-deception and self-excuse—the life of religion; but for many it is the begetter, the renewer and the guardian of such social usefulness as shall ever be theirs. For the deepest secret of the soul's social effectiveness lies just here—it has been laid hold of by an ideal which it knows to be real, and it is denied peace until that ideal is translated out of its own interior certainty into the structure of its world's life.

TWO SPECIFIC ISSUES

THE CHRISTIAN CRITIQUE OF COMMUNISM

THE CHRISTIAN AND COMPROMISE

THE CHRISTIAN CRITIQUE OF COMMUNISM

I. Agreements
>   1. The Dialectic Interpretation of History
>   2. The Necessity for Revolutionary Change
>   3. Radical Redistribution of Wealth
>   4. A Classless Society
>   5. The Material Conditions of Life

II. Divergencies
>   1. The Determinative Conditions of Human History
>   2. Methods in the Social Struggle
>   3. The Re-creative Principle in History
>   4. Apocalypticism and Human Nature
>   5. The Character of Ultimate Reality

III. The Deeper Issue

THE CHRISTIAN CRITIQUE OF COMMUNISM

I

At the very outset it may be well to mark off the areas of agreement between Marxism and Christianity, or at least the areas in which Christianity raises no necessary objection to Marxist doctrine. These areas are discovered to be larger and more important than many would expect.

1. Let it be said at once that Christianity finds nothing in the *dialectic interpretation of history* incompatible with its own view of the matter. The conception of advance in man's social development through the clash and mutual fructification of opposites is one which has had familiar place among Christian thinkers both in this and in a wider reference. Indeed, this principle of interpretation had its first notable exploitation in the thought of Heraclitus five hundred years before Christ, and had been subjected to careful analysis and criticism as to both its truth and its limitations in the *Phædo* a hundred years later. It reappears in our own day in somewhat modified form in Professor Hocking's 'principle of alternation.'[1] We have urged above that one of

[1] *Cf.* W. E. Hocking, *The Meaning of God in Human Experience*, Chap. XXVIII.

the more serious shortcomings of the modern outlook is its failure adequately to appreciate:

"the great cyclic movements of action and reaction in man's thought and man's progress which determine that periods of soaring idealism are succeeded by times of blunt realism; that romanticism and emotionalism and optimism make way for conservatism, dogmatism, reaction; that sophistication is usually followed by moral sterility; that high prosperity gives birth to superficiality, then arrogance, then profligacy, then disillusionment, then disgust with the world, then cynicism, then moral decline, and finally disintegration and retrogression."[2]

Christians need further to develop and articulate their own view of the dialectic of history.

2. Again, Christians should find no difficulty with the Marxist insistence upon *the necessity for revolutionary change.* Strange indeed is opposition here from a movement which was first thrust into the world in a vivid apocalyptic expectation, whose founder was executed as a dangerous revolutionary, which was early charged with turning the world upside down, which in every period of revival has given birth to tremendous energies for social regeneration. One of our own younger Christian thinkers, writing some years before the rise of contemporary Communism and without dependence upon Marx or Hegel, pointed out that:

"There is an inherent lethargy, entropy, conservatism in

[2] See above, p. 17.

human affairs (Is it not the reproduction in society of the characteristics of individual human nature?) which brings it about that when men try to preserve the *status quo,* they actually get stagnation; when they seek evolutionary change, they get a continuance of the *status quo;* when they strike for revolution, they achieve gradual advance."

Authentic Christianity has always generated powerful influences for social transformation. Indeed, we have suggested that true religion, by its inmost genius, is forever proclaiming the necessity for fundamental social change, and thrusting forth into the life of society concrete movements to bring that change to pass.

3. Nor does Christianity raise objection to the Marxist proposal for *radical redistribution of wealth.* Its own early life was one of the most notable concrete experiments in Communism in history. That experiment was inspired not merely by considerations of necessity but by spiritual currents welling from the profoundest centre of the Christian consciousness. Unwearying insistence upon a more equal possession of the physical goods of life and upon a radical sharing of those goods by their possessors would seem to be required of every Christian who has been faintly touched by the inner genius of his religion.

4. Again, Christianity finds no difficulty with the Marxist dream of a *classless society*—thoroughly congruous with Christianity's own ultimate goal.

5. Finally, Christians should not be too greatly

157

alarmed by what is often regarded as the keystone of the Marxist philosophy—*the theory of dialectical materialism*. This is a phrase of obscure meaning and dire associations for many who employ it. It cannot be too emphatically stressed that it has small part with traditional materialism—all that we mean when we think of that position as the arch-enemy of a theistic view of the world. Indeed, Marx developed his own doctrine in bitter criticism of the mechanism and fatalism of traditional materialism. His great faith was in man's freedom from mechanistic determination, man's power through creative activity to turn the course of history. To be sure Communist thinkers reveal a radical inconsistency at this point—an inconsistency made inevitable by the retention not only of the term but of many of its old associations. However, the governing conviction of the ruling view is clear enough—the assertion of man's power to control and remake material factors for his own purposes. Historically, materialism has implied a mechanistic fatalism; by contemporary Marxists this view is labelled 'mechanicism'; it is *one* of the two despised and unforgivable heresies, the other being religious idealism. To the Marxist, materialism means at most that matter is more fundamental (not more powerful) than mind, material circumstances than spiritual aspirations; often, it means merely that the material or economic circumstances of life condition men's lot and the development of their history. (The employment of so old a word with so altered a meaning is almost certainly an unhappy source of confusion.) The point has been made by Professor Sidney Hook that 'dialectical materialism' is "a philosophy held under other names by many who disavow" [3] Communist political interests altogether, for example by Professor Roy West Sellars in his *Evolutionary Naturalism*. Not infrequently, one would suspect it of drinking deeply of the pragmatism of William James. Professor Hook further reminds us that its fundamental metaphysical affinities are not with the materialistic atomism of Democritus, but with Aristotelianism—surely not a very forbidding enemy of Christianity in the light of classical Christian theology.

II

Where, then, can we locate the crucial divergencies between Marxism and Christianity, and so be enabled to formulate Christianity's challenge to Marxism? All have been implied in our examination of the Christian philosophy of history in the preceding chapter; those implications may be very briefly pointed out here. Let us examine five:

1. *The Determinative Conditions of Human History*. Marxism offers its theory of the *economic* determination of history. The dialectic movement of action and reaction in mankind's life which is so obvious to the

[3] Sidney Hook, *Journal of Philosophy*, Vol. 25, pp. 146-147.

acute student is interpreted purely in economic terms. Here Engels' oft-quoted statement is classic:

"The ultimate cause and great moving power of all important historic events is the economic development of society, changes in the modes of production and exchange."

To the suggestion of the economic determination of history, Christianity proffers an alternative interpretation—that of the *moral* determination of history. These two views are not necessarily completely antithetic, but in the practical philosophies which they beget, they may be and usually are incompatible. The Christian interpretation has occupied us in some detail above. We may summarize our understanding of it briefly as follows:

The ultimate factors and forces which surround mankind's life in the large and determine its advance and retreat—the conditions of its true progress—are ethical in character. Economic forces are determinative of human history, *ultimately,* in the measure that they are representative of, and the instruments of, moral realities. A sound appraisal of their significance can be had only through an understanding of the moral forces which condition and empower them.

The Christian conviction, while born of an initial intuition into the character of reality, receives abundant confirmation from fearless analysis of the brute facts of human history. To eyes alert to discern its deeper significance, the long story of mankind's pilgrimage reveals the structure of a moral order which surrounds human life, both individual and corporate, and forever reminds it of the essentially ethical framework within which it is set. Human freedom, social no less than personal, moves within fixed and inexorable limits which represent the moral structure of the universe. A too great defiance of the laws of that structure brings its inevitable penalty—in social conflict, confusion and disintegration. The fate of each succeeding empire and economy gives its clear testimony to the obdurate laws of social advance. Christianity is confirmed in its insight that the ultimately determinative conditions of human history *are* ethical, and that they will finally prevail.[4]

From this basic contrast two others follow:

2. *The Legitimate Methods in the Social Struggle.*

For the realization of its social goals, Marxism leans heavily upon the inevitability of the class struggle, and does not hesitate before any employment of violence which is likely to further its objectives. But, as we pointed out earlier in our discussion of the Christian logic of history, it is implicit in Christianity's certainty of the ethical unity of reality that it places confidence in no methods for the accomplishment of social change—however worthy the goal—which are not themselves consonant with the goal desired. To employ injustice, violence, ruthless coercion for the achievement of socially desirable ends, is to set loose in the world forces of evil which—the universe being a moral organism—are certain to take their toll from those who employ them and to qualify, and in some measure nullify, the good ends achieved.

[4] See above, pp. 111–120.

3. *The Re-creative Principle in Human History.*

Marxism conceives the development of social life as ultimately conditioned by economic factors; Christianity by moral forces. By the same token, Marxism places its confidence for the reconstruction of society and the achievement of the better life for men primarily in the reorganization of the economic order; Christianity primarily in the agency of creative persons. To be sure the contrast here is by no means absolute. It was Marx's great departure from traditional materialism that he affirmed men's power to influence their own destiny; there is much talk in Marxist writings about 'creative human activity.' But how far Marxism is from making its practical philosophy consistent with this belief, how far it is still actually under the dominance of the old view, is clearly revealed in its literature.[5] (This we should expect, since Marx himself, with all of his claims for men's capacities to effect change, lived in abstraction from dynamic human relationships and in ignorance of the inner souls of men, in the world of 'isms' and physical forces which dominate his thought.) The emphasis falls almost wholly upon 'forces,' 'systems,' 'isms.'

---

[5] So convinced an interpreter of Marxism as Sidney Hook, seeking to save it from this very charge, admits "that most of Marx's disciples have actually agreed with his critics—not perhaps in so many words—but as far as the objective intent of their interpretation goes." He then goes on to this amazing declaration: "A Charlemagne, a Mahomet, a George Washington or a Frederick II boasted the possession of no qualities so unique that other men could not have easily been found to lead the movements whose titular heads they were. Today the same can be said of Hitler or Gandhi. It is no exaggeration to maintain that if they had not been what they were, then, historically speaking, others would have been what they were." *Toward the Understanding of Karl Marx,* p. 165.

It is this which gives to Marxism its impression of incurable abstraction, its servitude to an artificial ideology. Like all abstract philosophies, it creates its own distinctive and rather esoteric vocabulary. To sink one's mind in the Marxist writings is to feel oneself removed from real life, from the simple but dynamic facts and relationships which actually characterize human experience as we all know it. This is part of its unhappy legacy from Hegel.

In this respect, Marxism falls into the error which vitiates many philosophies of history, whose inadequacy we noted earlier. Viewing history from the perspective of the impartial observer, they fasten attention upon general tendencies, the play of great impersonal forces, and interpret history in these terms, deterministically. Their conclusions appear fatalistic and pessimistic. They falsify the story because they have lost from their view the creative principle in history—the vision and life and influence of the individual person. Here is the force upon which Christianity places primary reliance for the gradual emancipation and improvement of society.

4. *The Validity of Apocalypticism and the Fundamental Character of Human Nature.*

Marxism prophesies the advent of 'the classless society.' It holds undiscourageable confidence in men's response to the promise of a better order, and in the perfectibility of human nature.

To a mature Christianity, this is the veriest romanticism. It is often claimed that Marxism is realistic, Christianity idealistic. But where in the whole gamut of contemporary thought can we detect such romantic idealism? With all its emphasis upon a philosophy of history, has Marxism learned nothing from the story of the human pilgrimage?

It may seem strange indeed that Christianity, itself born in a vivid apocalyptic hope, should bring strictures against a high eschatology. But the wisest Christianity has learned from its own past.[6] It knows that the perfect society is not to be seen in our world, by either divine intervention or human reconstruction. It knows that the classes which divide society are the inevitable fruit of tendencies deep within human nature, not the reverse. The abolition of the existing classes, however desirable, will have its final issue in a new stratification of society in which each group again seeks to impose its will on others. The ideal of a classless society is as chimerical as the vision of a perfect order on earth. Further, Christianity has learned that the forces which most require treatment for society's advance are lodged

[6] There is a Christian attack now being advanced against Marxism in terms of an alternative apocalypticism. Marxism is at fault, it is said, not in its apocalyptic expectation, but in its confidence in the action of men instead of the power of God. The two views are equally false. They misread the character of our world—one in its sentimental confidence in human nature, the other in its misrepresentation of the way in which God actually operates within human history.

Professor Sidney Hook denies that Marx and Engels, or their most intelligent contemporary followers, can be charged with such utopianism. But he admits that it characterizes the thought of great numbers who claim to be orthodox Marxists.

deep within each life, and will not be exorcised by any reordered system; they reappear and must be dealt with afresh in each generation and in every possible economy. In brief, Christianity knows something of *sin*.

5. *The Character of Ultimate Reality.*

We have come to feel before this that the deeper divergence between Marxism and Christianity is one of basic outlook, of ultimate certainty, of conviction of the structure of Reality. Marxism denies the reality of the Supernatural. Christianity stands or falls on its certain reality and its vital relevance to every aspect of human experience. We have just referred to the charge that "Marxism is realistic; Christianity idealistic." But what is 'the real'? That is the central issue.

A familiar vindication of Christian belief advances the argument that 'what ought to be true, must be true.' In contrast, Marxism claims to begin with 'what is.' However, the Christian apologetic which has proceeded from 'what ought to be' to 'what is' has never given an authentic statement; it has never claimed support from large numbers of Christians, nor from any for long periods. Christianity is not an argument from 'what ought to be' to 'what is.' It is an argument from 'what is' to 'what is.' Or, perhaps more significantly, from 'what IS' to 'what may be.' It reasons from what is indisputably real within the experience of a part of the totality of mankind to what is completely real in Ultimate Reality, and then on to what, on that account, might be completely REAL in the experience of all mankind. The Christian certainty does not concern something which is 'ideal' in contradistinction to the 'real'; but those things which are the most certain 'realities' we know.

Between the conception of society as a nexus of impersonal and mechanistic economic forces which determine the conditions and the outcome of mankind's life, and the conception of society as created and sustained and, in its ultimate destiny, guided by the moral Sovereign of Reality, there is, it will be agreed, a great gulf fixed.

III

These, and other, points of vital contrast between the Christian and the Marxist philosophies might be developed. But many who have not had opportunity or interest to define theoretical disagreements have sensed within themselves an instinctive distaste, yes distrust, of the Communist program which they hoped did not spring wholly from traditional or bourgeois prejudice; they hoped they were not deceived in their impression that it rose from somewhere near the heart of their Christian consciousness.

No, the line of cleavage between Christianity and Marxism is not to be drawn in terms merely of divergence in intellectual convictions. What leads Christianity to issue challenge to Marxism and, indeed, to

THE CHRISTIAN AND COMPROMISE

No problem is more perplexing to Christians, especially Christian ministers, in our day than the question of compromise. From all sides we hear the call to enlist in secular political and social movements. The objectives they seek are closely akin to our own ideals for a Christian society; we feel strong impulsion to join our resources to them. But the spirit and method by which they propose to reach these objectives are often utterly alien to what we have always conceived as the 'Christian method' of achieving the Christian goal. To throw ourselves into such movements seems to demand of us compromise from which we shrink. On the other hand, does not unwillingness to lend support involve us in compromise which, just because it is passive, may be even more blameworthy? This is our dilemma.

Our purpose in this essay is to seek guideposts for this specific perplexity. But behind it, is the far larger issue of the compromises required of Christians in *all* their relations within a thoroughly un-Christian society. Light upon the concrete problem may suggest principles to guide us in the wider area.

I

At the outset it will be well if we reach thorough understanding on a number of basic presuppositions.

These may seem very obvious; but failure fully to appreciate them is responsible for much unprofitable controversy. I shall mention four:

1. It is often said that the only alternative to compromise is 'asceticism.' If by 'asceticism' is meant an other-worldly abstention from the turmoils of humanity's life, it has no interest whatever for this discussion. Such abstention is not a living option for us. No, our problem is: "How far may a Christian become a partisan in secular social conflict, especially when such partisanship demands action definitely contrary to his Christian conscience?" The alternative to such participation is not other-worldliness. It is deliberate and resolute immersion in the area of conflict, *but* without partisan employment of the unethical procedures of the conflict. This is the meaning, and the only meaning, of Christian asceticism as we shall understand it.

2. As members of a society in which conflict and coercion are always covert if not overt facts, each of us at every moment is involved in compromise and is in some measure implicated in unethical social practices. This is the point relentlessly driven home upon the consciousness of our generation by Reinhold Niebuhr.[1] Its recognition is fundamental to any realistic consideration of our problem. However, it may readily lure

[1] Especially in his *Moral Man and Immoral Society* and *Reflections on the End of an Era.*

one into the fallacy that therefore *any* compromise is justified. Equally important is the recognition that there is wide variance in *degree* of involvement in compromise, both unwitting and conscious; and that here is the very heart of the matter. It would be absurd to affirm that a Salvation Army worker, merging his life wholly among the dispossessed and risking his livelihood with theirs, is as deeply involved in compromise as a pastor or teacher enjoying comfortable circumstance, assured income and protected future. With Christians the great perplexity is not, "Shall I permit myself to be involved in compromise?" but "What measure and what kind of compromise are permissible and inevitable?" Failure to recognize Niebuhr's point may encourage Christians who do *not* participate actively in social conflict in a wholly unjustified sense of self-righteousness. Failure to recognize the latter point may encourage Christians who *do* participate actively in social conflict in an equally dangerous type of self-deception.

3. There is no single "Christian course of personal action" equally binding upon all Christians at any one time. Ideally, there are diversities of gifts but the same spirit. Even more, there are diversities of vocation but the same objective. Conceivably two Christians, equally consecrated and equally within the line of God's purpose for them, might find themselves sharing the life

of groups on opposite sides of a social conflict. By the same token, two Christians, equally consecrated and equally within the line of God's purpose for them, might be discovered to be poles apart in the measure of their deliberate participation in such conflict—one throwing his energies fully into the conflict, the other withdrawn completely from partisan participation. Indeed, the Church will fulfill its total responsibility in the situation only as individual Christians do discharge widely varying and contrasted missions, all equally 'Christian.' The Christian ethic of personal procedure in the social struggle is relative to the capacities and the 'calling' of each individual.

4. There is no single definition of the limits of compromise which is equally valid under all circumstances, or even under closely similar circumstances at different periods. The Christian ethic is always relative, not only to the individual person, but to the specific occasion. More important for our present inquiry, the Christian ethic for *general* guidance, as far as it permits of determination at all, is relative to the existing situation of society and varies as that general situation varies.

II

This leads to the first of our guiding principles.

1. The measure of compromise permissible to Christians in their participation in the social struggle at any

time will depend upon what they conceive to be the general tendency within society at that moment; it will vary directly with what appears to be the prospect of a promising outcome of the general tendency. In general, when developments within society seem on the whole to be in the direction of the ultimate Christian ideal for society, Christians are called to a larger and larger measure of participation in secular political and social enterprises, with the inevitable attendant compromise. Contrariwise, when prevailing trends in society are away from the Christian objective, the Christian is required to practise a larger and larger measure of nonparticipation.

Another and more palatable application of the same principle would be: The measure of compromise permissible to Christians will depend upon the ethical quality of the particular political or social movement to which they feel drawn to join their energies; it will vary directly with the ethical ideal and consistency of that movement. When the purposes and procedures of the movement appear on the whole to be in line with the highest Christian ethic, Christians are called to a larger and larger measure of participation; and contrariwise. For example, in a day when the outlook for world fellowship was particularly dark in society's general drift, there might arise a secular movement vigorously promoting world fellowship along Christian lines. Obviously, Christians might be called to a large measure of participation in such a movement, even if considerable compromise were involved.

This principle will stir immediate criticism, on two scores:

a. It will be said that no one can tell when "the general tendency within society is in the direction of the ultimate Christian ideal." This is a matter of very difficult historic judgment; Christians might easily withhold their influence from a social development which, in the perspective of history, was discovered to be on the path of general social advance. These are, to be sure, baffling questions of personal judgment. But the objection has no weight here. For this is merely the difficulty Christians always face in attempting to appraise the ethical significance of any secular movement or leader, for instance every time they vote for public office.

b. It will be said that the principle smacks of the crassest opportunism. It is repugnant to every heroic impulse. Is it not precisely when the outlook for Christian ideals is darkest that Christians should throw themselves most completely into the social struggle, even at the cost of great compromise? Is it not precisely when the movements which are engaged in social struggle seem most devoid of ethical ideals and consistency that Christians should vigorously participate in them, at whatever compromise? This line of objection is natural, and it embraces a measure of truth. However, it is largely sentimental. There are other and far more complex considerations which must determine the issue for Christians. We shall come to them in our second general principle.

2. The measure of compromise permissible to Christians and their obligation to practise 'asceticism' is determined by the character of the Christian task in the world. Here, two considerations are paramount:[2]

a. *The dual character of human life.*

To this duality, we have referred repeatedly in the chapters which have preceded. Each man lives his life in a particular and transient setting—the age, the nation, the community, the circumstances in which he happens to have been born. These external factors determine in large measure his generation's and his own distinctive history. On the other hand, each man lives within that inner circle of personal experience and personal relationship which is a feature common to the existence of all the children of every age. Here centre a good half of the interests and concerns which occupy him; and here the social situation affects him but little.

So the Church finds men. So it must minister to them. The twofold character of their experience determines its responsibility and its message. More particularly, its pre-occupation with its prophetic task must not be permitted to unfit it for its pastoral responsibili-

[2] On the paragraphs which follow, see also above, pp. 130–133.

ties. Rather it must so discharge its mission to the pressing problems of the social scene that it is not in the smallest degree incapacitated for its mission to the profound and perennnial needs of personal life. Concretely, the Christian minister should be able to turn *instantaneously* from whatever social undertaking may be engaging him—platform speaking, organization, agitation, committee discussion—to conduct the funeral or to minister comfort for any needy human soul— capitalist, peasant, artisan, striker, hired scab. The Church must at all costs be faithful to its bounden duty to preserve its gift of grace and power and healing through all the ebb and flow of transient social circumstance.

b. The condemned state of human society.

After the same fashion, the Church's view of society is, as we have noted, twofold. It sees vividly the present issues of the social scene, and it has an indispensable message for their interpretation. The premises of this message we have sought to discover and outline. But the Church also knows that the pressing social problems of the moment are only the current forms in which the perennial and recurrent conflicts of man's corporate experience have taken temporary expression. They must be taken with utmost seriousness; but they must not be taken with a seriousness which destroys historic perspective. Just as the Church must remind individuals of the dual setting of their life, so it must forever remind

SUGGESTED READINGS

CHAPTER ONE

THE MESSAGE AND THE MAN OF TODAY

Allen, Frederick Lewis, *Only Yesterday.* 1931.
Berdyaev, Nicholas, *The End of Our Time.* 1933.
Horton, Walter M., *Theism and the Modern Mood.* 1930.
Jung, C. G., *Modern Man in Search of a Soul.* 1933.
Luccock, Halford C., *Contemporary American Literature and Religion.* 1934.
Mumford, Lewis, *Technics and Civilization.* 1934.
Niebuhr, Reinhold, *Moral Man and Immoral Society.* 1932.
—— *Reflections on the End of an Era.* 1934.
Randall, John Herman, Jr., *The Making of the Modern Mind.* 1926.
Sullivan, Mark, *Our Times.*
Tillich, Paul, *The Religious Situation* (tr. by H. R. Niebuhr). 1932.
Titterton, W. R., *Have We Lost God?* 1933.
Warnshuis, A. L. (Editor), *The Christian Message for the World Today.* 1933.

CHAPTER TWO

THE MESSAGE OF THE LIVING GOD

Berdyaev, Nicholas, *The End of Our Time.* 1933.
Bushnell, Horace, *Life and Letters.* 1905.
Croly, Herbert, *The Promise of American Life.* 1910.
Josephson, Matthew, *The Robber Barons.* 1934.
Jung, C. G., *Modern Man in Search of a Soul.* 1933.
Porter, Gene Stratton, *Laddie.* 1913.
Sullivan, Mark, *Our Times.*
Taylor, A. E., *The Faith of a Moralist.* 1930.
—— "The Vindication of Religion," in *Essays Catholic and Critical.*
Temple, William, *Nature, Man and God.* 1935.

Tillich, Paul, *The Religious Situation* (tr. by H. R. Niebuhr). 1932.

Vanamee, Mrs. Parker, *Vanamee*. 1930.

Van Dusen, Henry P., *The Plain Man Seeks for God*. 1933.

Whitehead, Arthur North, *Science and the Modern World*. 1925.

—— *Nature and Life*. 1934.

CHAPTER THREE

THE MESSAGE IN SOCIETY'S CRISIS

Bennett, John C., *Social Salvation*. 1935.

Berdyaev, Nicholas, *The End of Our Time*. 1933.

Brown, William Adams, *Is Christianity Practicable?* 1916.

Hobhouse, L. T., *Development and Purpose*. 1927.

Hocking, William Ernest, *Human Nature and Its Remaking*. 1923.

—— *The Meaning of God in Human Experience*. 1912.

Hook, Sidney, *Toward the Understanding of Karl Marx*. 1933.

Horton, Walter M., *Realistic Theology*. 1934.

James, William, *The Will to Believe*. 1912.

Johnson, F. Ernest, *The Church and Society*. 1935.

Martin, Hugh (Editor), *Christian Social Reformers of the Nineteenth Century*. 1927.

Niebuhr, Reinhold, *Moral Man and Immoral Society*. 1932.

—— *Reflections on the End of an Era*. 1934.

Royce, Josiah, *The Spirit of Modern Philosophy*. 1892.

Van Dusen, Henry P., *The Plain Man Seeks for God*. 1933.

Warnshuis, A. L. (Editor), *The Christian Message for the World Today*. 1933.

Whitehead, Arthur North, *Science and the Modern World*. 1925.

INDEX

INDEX

Abstraction, 33–67.

America, 3, 6, 18, 22, 46–59, 138–142.

America Finding Herself, 52 n.

American, typical, 9.

Amos, 118.

Apocalypticism, 163–165.

Aristotelianism, 159.

Arts, The, and religion, 144–145.

Asceticism, 172, 177, 183.

Augustus, 16.

'Barbarism, Return to,' 115.

Beauty, 36, 78, 83–84.

Behaviorism, 16.

Berdyaev, Nicholas, 67 n., 93 n., 94 n.

Blake, William, 85.

Browning, Robert, 86 n.

Buchan, John, 14 n.

Burt, Struthers, 21 n.

Bushnell, Horace, 82 n.

Business and abstraction, 36.

Century of Progress Exposition, 7.

Character and insight, 137–142.

Chartres Cathedral, 19.

Christian apologetics, 31.

"Christian Colleges," 48–49, 58.

Christian ethic and compromise, 174–180.

Christian faith, 25, 108 ff., 181.

Christian logic of history, The, 102, 107–133.

Christian message, 25, 148; of God, 67–88; to society, 98–133.

Christian Message for the World Today, The, 94 n.

Christian Social Reformers of the Nineteenth Century, 146 n.

Christian strategy in society, The, 130–133, 181–183.

Christian thought, 14.

Christianity, 13, 25, 85, 113; and

Communism, 122 n., 155–167; and Apocalypticism, 163–165.

Christianity and compromise, 171–183.

Church, The, 56, 70, 91, 119, 131–132, 174, 177–178; and modern thought, 13–15, 31–33; in the modern age, 30–33, 95; and reform, 144–146; and society, Chap. 3, 178–183.

Civil War, the American, 122.

Classless society, 101, 157.

Clutton-Brock, A., 44.

Coercion, 121, 172.

Coleridge, Hartley, 147 n.

Communism, 24, 94, 96, 122 n.; Christian critique of, 155–167.

Compromise and the Christian, 171–183.

Conscience, 80–83.

Croly, Herbert, 52 n.

Culture, 9, 17–18, 36, 47.

Debs, Eugene V., 149.

Democracy, 92.

Democratic Party, 48.

Democritus, 159.

'Demonic' interpretation of history, 105–107, 111, 129.

Depression, The, 9, 20, 53, 117–120, 138–142.

Determinism, 105, 115, 129.

Dialectic interpretation of history, 155–156.

Dialectical materialism, 158–159.

Economic determination of history, 111, 159–161.

Education, 17, 47–49, 57–59; and abstraction, 35.

End of Our Time, The, 67 n., 93 n., 94 n.

Engels, 160, 164 n.

Essays Catholic and Critical, 78 n.

INDEX

INDEX

INDEX

United States, 46–64.
Universe, 62, 68, 78–80.

Vanamee, 83 n.
Vanamee, Mrs. Parker, 83 n.
Victorian Era, 46.
Vision, gift of personal religion, 133–134.
Voltaire, 149.

Washington, George, 51.
Wealth, redistribution of, 157.
Wesleyan Revival, 14.
Whitehead, A. N., 33, 34 n., 36 n., 37 n., 134, 167.
Will to Believe, The, 104 n.
Wilson, Woodrow, 148.
Wordsworth, William, 84, 167.
World War, 9, 20, 91, 122, 148.